## Chinese Literature

Chinese literature has a long, distinctive hi<br>
part in shaping the cultural identity of th<br>
provides a window into human relations<br>
and philosophy at any given time in C<br>
illustrated introduction takes the reader t. ....... .... Chinese literary
tradition from ancient times to the twentieth century, exploring poetry,
opera, drama, novels, short stories, the modern media and the authors who
created these cultural treasures.

## Introductions to Chinese Culture

The thirty volumes in the Introductions to Chinese Culture series provide accessible overviews of particular aspects of Chinese culture written by a noted expert in the field concerned. The topics covered range from architecture to archaeology, from mythology and music to martial arts. Each volume is lavishly illustrated in full color and will appeal to students requiring an introductory survey of the subject, as well as to more general readers.

*Yao Dan et al*

# CHINESE LITERATURE

CAMBRIDGE UNIVERSITY PRESS
Cambridge, New York, Melbourne, Madrid, Cape Town,
Singapore, São Paulo, Delhi, Tokyo, Mexico City

Cambridge University Press
The Edinburgh Building, Cambridge CB2 8RU, UK

Published in the United States of America by Cambridge University Press,
New York

www.cambridge.org
Information on this title: www.cambridge.org/9780521186780

Originally published by China Intercontinental Press as
*Chinese Literature* (9787508515861) in 2010

© China Intercontinental Press 2010

This updated edition is published by Cambridge University Press
with the permission of China Intercontinental Press under
the China Book International programme .

For more information on the China Book International programme, please visit
http://www.cbi.gov.cn/wisework/content/10005.html

Cambridge University Press retains copyright in its own contributions
to this updated edition

© Cambridge University Press 2012

First published 2012

Printed and bound in China by C&C Offset Printing Co., Ltd

*A catalogue record for this publication is available from the British Library*

ISBN   978-0-521-18678-0 Paperback


NOT FOR SALE IN THE PEOPLE'S REPUBLIC OF CHINA (EXCLUDING
HONG KONG SAR, MACAU SAR AND TAIWAN)

# **Contents**

# Foreword

The brilliant tradition of ancient Chinese literature is still being appreciated today. Music and painting were also highly developed in ancient China, but most ancient musical scores have been lost and most of the paintings surviving today are from the time of the Song Dynasty (960–1279) and later. Only literature, the songs and myths our forefathers created, have been left. The world of the Zhou Dynasty (1046–221 BC) depicted in *The Book of Songs* remains vivid today. Reading *The Book of Songs* and works by Pre-Qin philosophers reveals principles and ethics which, over the span of three thousand years, have shaped the cultural identity of the Chinese people.

Relatively clear records survive from the Zhou Dynasty, articulating the ideals of Chinese society at that time, governed by classics, music, and a feudal codes of ethics - to which sages often aspired in later eras. The ideal political pattern in ancient China was not rule by force, but by the implementation of education. The scholars, a social stratum between senior officials and the common people in ancient China, played the role of educating commoners. According to the political system of the Zhou Dynasty, the nobles ranked below the emperor. The nobles of the upper stratum were senior officials. The nobles of the lower stratum were the scholars. The scholars were further divided into the upper scholars, the middle scholars and the lower scholars. The earliest literature in China was the literature of the scholars. Scholars collected folk songs from among the people, arranged them and polished them and presented them

A painted scroll of Chinese poets through the ages.

to the emperor so that he could read the social customs and understand the aspirations of the people. These folk songs became the poems included in the section of "Guofeng" ("Folk Songs") in *The Book of Songs,* the earliest anthology of Chinese poetry. Poems written for the ancestral shrine and sacrificial rites constituted the section "Song" ("Sacrificial Songs") and historical records became the section "Ya" ("Court Hymns"). But Chinese literature concerned human relationships and everyday life as well as political education. Moreover, it was closely related to the spiritual life of the people.

Traditionally, the Chinese people strive for the harmony of man with nature, firmly believing that the foundation of human relationships and everyday life lies in communion with heavenly principles. Great writers concerned themselves with the whole universe, history, and the tribulations of the people. Great thinkers of the Spring and Autumn and the Warring States Period (770–221 BC) cherished lofty aspirations of bringing prosperity to the country and a better life to the people. Confucius, Mencius, Laozi, and Zhuangzi traveled between various states promoting their views and thoughts on life and good government. By the time of the Han Dynasty (206 BC–220 AD), Sima Qian, writing *Records of the Historian* with the aim of fully "exploring the interaction between Heaven and Man and giving a complete

and authoritative account of the historical changes of the past and present," carried this forward. Li Bai and Su Shi of the Tang (618–907) and the Song dynasties, great poets worthy of the line "Heaven has made us talents, we're not made in vain," talked and danced with the sun, the moon, the mountains, and the rivers, yet they were agonized with concern for the people when writing their poems. These are among the great splendors of Chinese literature.

From the time of the Yuan Dynasty (1206–1368), the morale of the Chinese people was seriously dampened. As a result, the pattern of Chinese literature altered too. Though scholars before the Yuan Dynasty spoke for the people and concerned themselves with the life of the people, their words and writings were intended for the monarchs and the ruling class. However, from the Yuan Dynasty onwards, scholars started to write plays and popular stories for the common people so that they could relax when they were not working. During this period, the "comic spirit" in Chinese literature made its first appearance, such as in the work of the playwright Guan Hanqing. Aside from this, the direct influence literature exerted upon people's everyday life was also increased when popular novels were widely read among the people. The Chinese people's understanding of "faithfulness" and "righteousness" even today comes mainly from the novels *Three Kingdoms* and *Outlaws of the Marsh*. In the mid-eighteenth century, *A Dream of Red Mansions*, an independent and scholarly novel influenced by Western literary concepts, was published. Following the history of several families, considering the fate of women and exploring the idea that "life is but a dream," it captured the attention of the readers of that time and later generations. It is thought to be the greatest Chinese novel.

The early twentieth century saw the outburst of the "May 4th" New Culture Movement in China. An omni-directional transformation of Chinese literature took place, including the transformation of literary ideas, content and language, and even the relationship between Chinese literature and world literature. From this time a new period of modern Chinese literature unfolded. The modern idea of reshaping "national character" brought forward and promoted by Lu Xun and Zhou Zuoren ran through the entire course of modern Chinese literature. By writing a few short stories and numerous essays, Lu Xun created portraits of the Chinese nation, moulding the self-image of the Chinese people within a few decades. After this, a multitude of novelists, essayists, dramatists, poets, literary theorists and critics explored the themes of cultural innovation, national liberation and class warfare, giving responses to social reality with different literary forms.

In the 1940s and 1950s, significant changes in Chinese society led to important changes in the Chinese literature pattern. Literature was given more prominence in social and political life. Cherishing the ideal of building an independent nation, most writers greeted the "New Times" with great warmth. To write epic works that would reflect the "great times" became the responsibility of writers with lofty ideals. With the ending of the ten barren years of the Cultural Revolution (1966–1976), a new historical period of contemporary literature was ushered in. This provided a new opportunity for contemporary literature and the policy of "letting a hundred flowers blossom and a hundred schools of thought contend" was restored as the guiding principle in literary writing. Literary circumstances in the new era were completely changed. With the wide introduction of China's market economy, China's consumption began to boom and with it popular culture. Under the impact of a market economy, writers began to be aware of the commodity properties of literary creation, publication and distribution. As a result, many writers began to take part in the more profitable writings of "sub-literature." As an important branch of "sub-literature," China's film and television literature and cyber literature has become an important branch of Chinese literary creation and is developing rapidly.

# *The Book of Songs*

## The Earliest Anthology of Poetry

*ook of Songs*, the earliest anthology of poetry in China, is one of the most significant survivals in Chinese literature. It contains 305 poems written in a period of almost 500 years, starting from the early years of the Western Zhou through to the mid-Spring and Autumn Period (c. eleventh to sixth century BC). Today, Confucius is generally believed to be the compiler of the book. In terms of origin, the poems included in *The Book of Songs* come from the following three sources: The first is called "advice poems." When an emperor of the Western Zhou Dynasty held court, ministers and royal princes offered poems to him to make implicit remonstrances or to sing his praises. The second source is called "folk songs and ballads." Official collectors of folk songs and ballads from the Western Zhou and other co-existing states went into villages to collect folk songs and ballads which were popular among the ordinary people. The rest of the poems included in *The Book of Songs* are songs that were specially used for sacrificial rites and on banquet occasions. These songs were written by "professional" writers such as court official musicians or shamans and official historians.

Accordingly, all the poems included in *The Book of Songs* fall into different sections. The poems that come from the people belong to the section of "Feng" (ballads or folk songs), the advice poems dedicated to the emperor belong to the section of "Ya" (court hymns or odes), and those used for sacrificial rites and banquet occasions belong to "Song" (sacrificial songs). Originally, "Feng," "Ya" and "Song" were different genres of music. "Feng" referred to the local music of different states. "Ya," meaning orthodox, referred to court music. "Song," along with singing and dancing, was slow tempo dance music mainly used for sacrificial

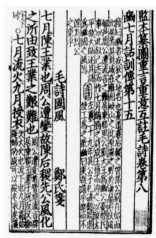

*The Book of Songs*, the block-printed edition of the Song Dynasty, collection of the National Library of China.

Bells were the main ceremonial musical instruments for sacrificial ceremonies and banquet occasions of Pre-Qin kings and aristocrats.

ceremonies. Due to the differences between the music and its purposes, the three sections of *The Book of Songs*, "Feng," "Ya" and "Song," bear some inconsistencies both in content and aesthetic style. "Ya" and "Song" are solemn and over-elaborate, while "Feng," also known as "Guofeng" (folk songs of fifteen regions), is soul-stirring and passionate. However, taking into consideration the time of the Western Zhou Dynasty when *The Book of Songs* was written, politics and culture were centered on the nobility. The common people had very little personal freedom, let alone the time to write. For this reason, the poems in the section of "Guofeng" in *The Book of Songs* were still works written by the nobility, though sometimes they served as spokesmen for the rustic and common people.

# "Folk Songs of Fifteen Regions" ("Guofeng")

When talking about *The Book of Songs*, Chinese readers are often actually referring to the section of "Guofeng" in *The Book of Songs*. The love poems included in "Guofeng" are rather diverse and colorful: some are impassioned, some unbridled, and some simple and unadorned but refreshing. But all these love poems are the "true voice of the mind" with the least sign of affectation or decadence.

The opening poem of *The Book of Songs*, "Crying Ospreys: Zhou and the South" in "Guofeng," is about love. It reads:

*Merrily the ospreys cry, / On the islet in the stream. / Gentle and graceful is the girl, / A fit wife for the gentleman.*

These lines are perhaps among the most famous in Chinese poetry. Assuming that the birds translated here as "osprey" mated for life and were always seen together, the sight of these love birds naturally touched the poet's longing for his sweetheart. Subsequently, he began to chant: "Merrily the ospreys cry, / On the islet in the stream. / Gentle and graceful is the girl, / A fit wife for the gentleman." Through these lines, the poet expresses his longing for a girl. Unable to sleep or eat, the poet only hopes that one day he can win over the girl's heart.

The love poems included in *The Book of Songs* are varied in content and form, but unrequited love is a consistent theme. The poems with this theme are also the most touching and inspiring. "Crying Ospreys" is one example. Another is "The Reeds: The Social Mode of Qin," which reads:

*The reeds are luxuriant and green, / The white dew has turned to frost. / My beloved so dear to me / Is somewhere beyond the waters. / Upriver I search for him, / The way is arduous and long. / Downriver I search for him, / He seems to be in the middle of the waters.*

The poet's poetic thoughts start with the reeds. "Man is but a reed," said the French philosopher Blaise Pascal, "the weakest in nature, but he is a

**Ospreys**
Ospreys, sometimes known as sea hawks, are water birds. Zhu Xi, a Confucian scholar of the Song Dynasty, wrote that ospreys "are noted for their faithfulness in love. If one of a couple dies, the other will be so overwhelmed with anxiety and depression that it will starve itself to death." As a Confucian scholar, Zhu Xi focuses on the "faithfulness" of the ospreys - once one of the couple dies, the other will cease to be too. The orthodox school of Confucianism since the Han Dynasty has accepted that *Crying Ospreys: Zhou and the South* is a poem extolling the virtues of the consorts of the Western Zhou emperors. Zhu Xi is actually demanding women to be faithful to their husbands. A major feature of the Confucian school of the Song Dynasty was that women were expected to remain unmarried after their husbands' death or to commit suicide after their husbands' death or in defense of their chastity. Of course, the faithfulness of the ospreys in "Crying Ospreys" is a "transitory interpretation" made by later generations. The original intention of the poet is more likely to have been to express longing and affection for the one he loved.

thinking reed." In the poem, the reeds serve as a symbol for the fragility of human beings. The soft and gentle reeds by the waters swayed in the autumn wind. It looks as if the poet's sweetheart is right there across the water. But when she tries to get there and reach him, she finds that the way is arduous and long and, moreover, her sweetheart always seems to be in the middle of the water, completely unattainable. This poem vividly conveys the sadness caused by a person's longing for his or her sweetheart. The desolate and misty autumn scene is resonant with the poet's feelings.

*The Social Mode of Bin* (detail), a painting by Ma Hezhi of the Song Dynasty. "In the Seventh Month: The Social Mode of Bin" is a famous poem on farming, depicting scenes of farmers' labor during the four seasons. This painting is an artistic adaptation of the poem itself. It represents a joyful banquet scene at the end of the lunar year.

Of course, "Guofeng" covers a lot of ground in terms of content. There are also many poems concerning farming, war and feudal labor. "In the Seventh Month: The Social Mode of Bin" is a famous poem about the life of the farmers. It describes the farmers' assiduous work throughout the year.

In comparison with "Ya" and "Song," the language used in "Guofeng" is closer to the spoken language, and the four-character lines, which are more often grave and rigid in "Ya" and "Song," become lively and dynamic in "Guofeng." In "Guofeng," there are many beautiful lines, which are either soul-stirring and broad-minded or profound and far-reaching in meaning.

# The Epic of the Western Zhou People

Scholars appreciate the "epic quality and style" of *The Book of Songs*. So they hold some of the poems in "Da Ya" ("Greater Odes") in high esteem. The five poems in "Da Ya," namely "In the Beginning Who Gave Birth to Our People?" ("Shengmin"), "Duke Liu" ("Gongliu"), "In Long Trains Ever Increasing Grow the Gourds" ("Mian"), "Great Is God" ("Huangyi"), and "The Illustration of Illustrious Virtue" ("Daming"), are regarded as the national epics of the Western Zhou people. In the West, the concept of an "epic" was first put forward by Aristotle, and the representative works are the two epic poems entitled *Iliad* and *Odyssey* attributed to Homer. Although these five poems cannot really be compared to the epics by Homer, by giving an account of the mythology of heroes, legends and historical tales at the beginning of the Western Zhou, these five poems are imbued with an epic quality and style. They tell the stories of how the Western Zhou people fight against and finally triumph over the

Significant sites of the Western Zhou Dynasty.

A portrait of Hou Ji, ancestor of the Zhou people.

Yin Dynasty (the later period of the Shang Dynasty). Each of the sovereigns described in the poems has his own distinguishing features: Hou Ji is good at farming, Duke Liu is honest, simple and upright, Ancient Duke Danfu is a man of foresight with pioneering spirit, King Wen is renowned for his virtues, and King Wu unifies the whole country by force and meritorious military service. Though they were written in the early years of the Western Zhou Dynasty, these poems had been circulating among the Western Zhou people for quite some time and, consequently, the influence of mythology in these poems is discernible. With simple imagination, the ancient sages portrayed their ancestors as half-humans and half-gods.

"In the Beginning Who Gave Birth to Our People?" tells the life story of Hou Ji, the first ancestor of the Western Zhou people. Jiangyuan, Hou Ji's mother, stepped in a god's footprint, and she conceived and gave birth to a child. This child was Hou Ji. After Hou Ji was born, his mother thought that this child of dubious background was an ill omen. She decided to abandon him. First she abandoned him on the road, hoping that oxen and sheep would tread on him. But the oxen and sheep made a detour with extreme caution to avoid treading on him. Then she abandoned him on the cold ice. But birds covered him with their wings to prevent him from dying of cold. Miraculously, he survived and grew up. When Hou Ji grew up, he became an expert at farming and taught his clansmen how to plough and sow. It was then that his clansmen made their home in Tai. Hou Ji's great grandson Duke Liu, a kind and honest man, then led his clansmen to move to Bin. After this, King Wen was born. By this time, the Western Zhou people had become an extremely powerful nation.

"Great Is God" tells about the story of how King Wen leads an expedition against the state of Mi and the state of Chong. "The Illustration of Illustrious Virtue," written in a lively style, focuses on King Wu's expedition against the Shang Dynasty. King Wu defeats the Shang troops which are superior in number. The war is graphically portrayed in just dozens of words. The lines "The troops of Yinshang, / Were collected like a forest" give a vivid description of the multitude and menace of the Shang troops. The following lines "The wilderness of Muye spread out extensive; / Bright shone the chariots of sandal; / The teams of bays, black-maned and white-bellied, galloped along; / The Grand-Master Shangfu, / Was like an eagle on the wing, / Assisting King Wu, / Who at one onset smote the great Shang. / That morning's encounter was followed by a clear bright [day]" can serve as a description of King Wu's army ready for fight and his tension and vigilance when facing the enemy troops. The spectacular image of Grand-Master Shangfu, who is portrayed as an eagle on the wing, foretells the final victory of the Western Zhou troops.

*Scroll on the Departing Chariot*, by Ma Hezhi of the Song Dynasty, represents the triumphant return of the Zhou armies.

It can be argued that the poems in "Da Ya" of *The Book of Songs* represent epics about the Western Zhou heroes. Yet there is a world of difference between these and the works of Homer: the epics attributed to Homer are of a more narrative style, while the epics in "Da Ya" are of a more lyrical style. Homer's epics were widely circulated and sung among the people by minstrels and were handed down by word of mouth with frequent modifications. The epics about the Western Zhou people were written by official historians and musicians and were to be chanted when they offered sacrifices to their ancestors. The basic content of the Western Zhou epics remained more static.

As regards their pursuit of poetic spirit, there are some further differences between *The Book of Songs* and Homer's epics. Homer's epics were imbued with the spirit of adventure and exploration. Though Odysseus's return home was the main plot of *Odyssey*, Homer gave a more elaborate description of Odysseus's adventurous experiences, which can be understood

The *Gui* Vessel of Heavenly Conquest, Western Zhou, with seventy-eight characters inscribed at its base, depicts the sacrificial ceremony hosted at the "Heavenly Chamber" after King Wu of Zhou exterminated the Shang Dynasty.

as man's struggles against, and in, nature. What is recorded in *The Book of Songs* is how the Western Zhou people built up a civilization of their own through their cordial and harmonious coexistence with nature. The Western Zhou people were more sentimentally attached to a peaceful, friendly and harmonious rural life. The sole aim of warfare, which came to them some time later, was either to drive out invading enemies or to revolt against tyranny.

# Prose Writings of Various Schools of Thought during the Spring and Autumn and the Warring States Period

## Models for Prose Writings

During the Spring and Autumn and the Warring States Period (770–221 BC), China gradually sank into war and chaos. "Sages do not arise, the various lords are debauched. Unemployed scholars debate unreasonably." With the decline of the royal court of the Zhou Dynasty, ducal states appeared in quick succession and were beleaguered by warfare. Unemployed scholars toured various states to publicize their ideas. These scholars put their ideas and thoughts in writing and we call these writings the "prose writings of various schools of thought during the Spring and Autumn and the Warring States Period." The debates among the pre-Qin Dynasty scholars were lively and dynamic, bringing about the contention of various schools of thought. Among these scholars, some were politicians, some were philosophers, some orators, and some were field specialists. Some scholars, such as Confucianists, Legalists and Mohists, spread their doctrines with the intention that rulers might use their thoughts to govern the country; some others, such as

Banquet Copper Pot of the Warring States Period, collection of the Palace Museum, Beijing, with engravings of land and water attacks, vividly captures the battle scenes of the period.

Laozi and Zhuangzi of the Taoist school, were only interested in expressing ideas and their own understanding of contemporary politics and society. It was a period in the history of China when people enjoyed spiritual liberty and when people's minds were emancipated to the full, comparing well with the golden age of classical Greek philosophy. It was an age of wise men. All questions and doubts were left open. Different scholars stuck to their own views on how each ducal state should be governed. As opinions on public affairs advocated by some schools were put forth with the objective to win over the rulers, debates were called. Poetry excels in conveying people's emotions. But, prose, which excels in reasoning, reached a new stage at this period. The prose writings of this period are rich in literary grace, teeming with not only philosophical wisdom, but also vivid metaphors, rich imagination and concern for the life of people. In terms of literary merits, the prose of the Confucian school and the Taoist school is believed to be the best of all.

# *Tao Te Ching*

*Tao Te Ching*, also known as *Laozi* or *Classic of the Way and Virtue*, is usually attributed to Laozi. Laozi, whose family name was Li and given name Dan, was the founder of Taoism. He was a native of the State of Chu of the Spring and Autumn Period and was born no later than 470 BC. As he was part of the social stratum between senior officials and the common people, he advocated the political thought "So long as I 'do nothing,' the people will of themselves be transformed. / So long as I love quietude, the people will of themselves go straight." *Tao Te Ching*, consisting of eighty-one chapters, falls into two sections, the first one being *Tao Ching* (*Classic of the Way*) and the second one *Te Ching* (*Classic of the Virtue*).

*Tao Te Ching* has 5,000 words. The word "Tao" is mentioned over 70 times in the book. Laozi was the first person who put forward the concept of Tao and regarded it as the supreme realm of philosophy. "The Tao that can be spoken of is not the eternal Tao." Tao is the origin of the universe. Viewed in the light of this concept, *Tao Te Ching* reveals that a number of Chinese people living during the Spring and Autumn Period had reached abstract thinking. In addition, Laozi is also a naturalist. He holds that since the Way of Heaven follows the

A portrait of Laozi.

course of nature and non-action, people should also conform to the Way of Heaven. Therefore, he takes the concept of "through actionless activity all things are duly regulated" and "a small state with a sparse population" as his political ideal. What he is concerned with is how to solve various disputes between people, how to guide people's activities to follow the naturalness and spontaneity of the "Tao" and how to make people's life free from political interference. "The government of the sage," which he praises highly, lies in

*Refrain from exalting capable men, so that the people shall not compete. / Refrain from valuing rare goods, so that the people shall not steal. / Refrain from displaying anything which arouses desires, so that the people's heart will not be disturbed. / Therefore the government of the sage lies in: / Simplifying the people's minds, / Filling their bellies, / Weakening their ambitions, / Strengthening their bones, / And always keeping the people innocent of knowledge and desires.*

"The sage" is the most perfect being in the mind of Taoists. But the personality of "the sage" in the mind of the Taoists differs from that of the Confucian school. "The sage" of the Confucian school is the model of men of virtue, whereas "the sage" of the

Taoist school identifies himself with what is natural and expands his internal life, taking "non-essentialness and motionless" and "non-competition" as the ideal way of life. So, the Taoist sage manages affairs by "non-action." "Non-action" as expressed in *Tao Te Ching* actually means not to act willfully, not to pursue selfish ends assiduously, but to abandon all of one's personal considerations and schemes and act in accordance with the principles of Heaven and Earth. In spite of all this, we can also find some inconsistencies in *Tao Te Ching*. Lu Xun pointed out that Laozi "sometimes has indignant remarks though he refrains from having a big mouth, and still cherishes the wish to govern the world though he strongly advocates non-action." Laozi's "indignant" remarks are as follows:

*When the Great Tao is abandoned, / The doctrines of benevolence and righteousness will come to light. / When knowledge and wisdom appear, / Great hypocrisy will also emerge. / When a family falls into dispute, / Filial piety and parental affection to children will be advocated. / When a country falls into disorder, / There will be loyal ministers.*

Laozi maintains that the metaphysical "Tao" is absolute and eternal, while everything dialectical is relative and changeable:

*Tao Te Ching.*

*Laozi on an Ox*, by Chao Buzhi of the Song Dynasty, collection of the Palace Museum, Beijing. Legend has it that Laozi realized the decadency of the Zhou Dynasty and disappeared to far-off lands on the ox's back.

*Therefore, by opposing each other, / Existence and nonexistence come into being, / Difficult and easy form themselves, / Long and short are distinct, / High and low contrast, / Sound and voice harmonize, / Front and back emerge.*

Relativism as expressed in the lines cited above is another principal theme running through *Tao Te Ching*. Moreover, these lines also disclose Laozi's perseverance. It is impossible for him to stick to non-action forever. As far as appearances go, he spares no effort in elaborating the relationship between existence and nonexistence, long and short, and black and white, yet in his heart he is also paying attention to the government of the country.

The language of *Tao Te Ching* is concise. Many lines from *Tao Te Ching*, such as the ones cited above - "Therefore, by opposing each other, / Existence and nonexistence come into being" - have become very popular maxims. There are also many lines in the book that resemble the undulating metre and rhyme scheme which is particular to *The Book of Songs*. The following is an example:

*He who knows the masculine but keeps to the feminine, is ready to be the ravine under Heaven. / Being the ravine under Heaven, he is not parted from constant "De" (Virtue). / He returns to the simple state, like an infant. / He who knows the white (glory) but keeps to the black (obscure), is ready to be the (divination) instrument of under Heaven. / Being the instrument of under Heaven, he rests upon constant "De," / He returns to the ultimate truth.*

# The Analects

Laozi advocates the other-worldly thoughts that "all things are duly regulated through "non-action." Unlike Laozi, Confucius (c. 551–479 BC) was one who "knows it's no use, but keeps on doing it." On the assumption that society in ancient times during the reign of Yao, Shun, King Wen and King Wu of the Zhou Dynasty was the ideal society for the people, Confucius tried hard to exert influence on the leaders of various states with his own doctrines in the hope of helping them return to the society of the antiquity, the politics of which was characterized by good government and prevalence of justice. The family name of Confucius is Kong and his name is Qiu, style name Zhongni. A native of the State of Lu, Confucius was at one time the Minister of Public Works and the Minister of Justice of the State of Lu. He also toured various countries in the late Spring and Autumn Period. But he had a difficult life, "looking crestfallen like a homeless, wandering dog." In his later years, he started his teaching career. Confucius had 3,000 pupils, 72 of whom were outstanding and renowned, well versed in all Six Arts—ceremony, music, archery, charioteering, writing, and mathematics. Confucius, as he said of himself, only "transmitted what was taught to me without making up anything of my own." After he returned to the State of Lu in his later years, he concentrated on revising and compiling the literary works of ancient China, including *Collection of Ancient Texts* (also known as *The Book of Documents*), *The Book of Songs*, *The Book of Changes*, *The Spring and Autumn Annals*, *The Record of Rites*, and *The Record of Music*. Confucius' words were mainly recorded by his pupils in *The Analects*. The image of Confucius is very distinctive though *The Analects* is a work written in the style of discourse. "The uncommon grace of Confucius is well shown in his maxims." When he was a child, Confucius was poor and humble. As an adult, he was made the Minister of Public Works. Later he resigned his government post and left the State of Lu to tour various countries. During the period after

A portrait of Confucius.

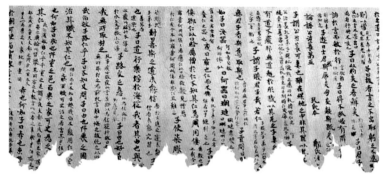

Surviving pages of the Tang Dynasty *The Analects* annotated by Zheng Xuan.

he left the State of Lu, he had a hard time—he "was dismissed from the State of Qi, driven out of the State of Song and the State of Wei and ran into trouble between the State of Chen and the State of Cai." But throughout his life he never regretted his aspirations. He worked indefatigably to carry forward the cause of the sages and pioneered a profound learning. Sima Qian of the Han Dynasty, the greatest historian of China, thus commented on Confucius in his "Confucius" in *Records of the Historian*, "One of the songs says, 'The great mountain, I look up to it! The great road, I travel it!' Although I cannot reach him, my heart goes out to him. When I read the works of Confucius, I try to see the man himself." Generally speaking, this comment expresses most Chinese intellectuals' attitude towards Confucius since the Han Dynasty.

*The Analects* is a record of Confucius' words and deeds. The language of *The Analects* is succinct, refined and profound. The gist of Confucius' remarks, namely "benevolence (perfect virtue)" and "ritual (propriety)," is in the first place directed at the sovereign. "Do not do to others what you would not like yourself. Then there will be no feelings of opposition to you, whether it is the affairs of a State that you are handling or the affairs of a Family (ruling clan)." Here the persons who handle the affairs of a State refer to dukes or princes of the State and the

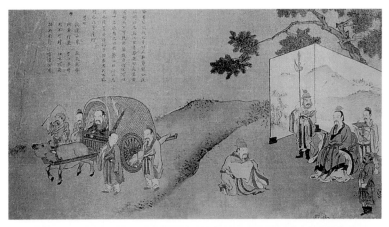

*The Holy Trace* (detail), Ming Dynasty, depicts Confucius touring the kingdoms, receding and amending the *Songs*, and teaching his disciples.

persons who handle the affairs of a ruling clan refer to senior officials. It is obvious that this requirement is aimed at the rulers. "To subdue one's self and return to propriety (Zhou rites)" is "perfect virtue." "To love men" is "perfect virtue." Remarks on "ritual" are as follows: "To look at nothing in defiance of ritual, to listen to nothing in defiance of ritual, to speak of nothing in defiance of ritual, never to stir hand or foot in defiance of ritual."

"Ritual" is at the same time a set of systems and social norms. When treating the people, "Govern them by moral force, keep order among them by ritual and they will keep their self-respect and come to you of their own accord." It is natural that people will have a proper sense of honor and disgrace if they are kept within the bounds of ritual and educated by virtue.

Though *The Analects* is a record of the words and deeds of Confucius and his disciples, the characters are vividly portrayed. The image of Yan Yuan (named Hui, styled Ziyuan), Confucius' favorite disciple, spreads far and wide through the ages in the lines of Confucius' profuse praises, "Incomparable indeed was Hui! A handful of rice to eat, a gourd-full of water to drink, living in a mean street—others would have found it unendurably depressing, but to Hui's cheerfulness it made no difference at all. Incomparable indeed was Hui." In addition, of all Confucius' disciples, Yan Yuan has the greatest love for learning and is a man of reputable character. He "never vented his wrath upon the innocent nor let others suffer for his faults. Unfortunately, the span of life allotted to him by Heaven was short, and he died." Each of Confucius' disciples has their own distinctive features: Zilu is outspoken and straightforward, Zigong has a ready tongue, and Zeng Xi (style name Dian) is free from vulgarity. When standing by Confucius' side in attendance upon him, "The attitude of Zilu was one of impatient energy, bold and soldierly; that of Ran You and of Zigong was free in manner and fluent in speech." Each of their individual personalities is manifested in full: "Once when Zilu, Zeng Xi, Ran You and Gongxi Hua were seated in attendance upon their Master" when they talk about their aspirations in "Book Eleven" of *The Analects*: Zilu gives a prompt and confident reply, while Zeng Xi is the last one to give his reply. Zeng Xi's reply is, "At the end of spring, with the dress of the season all complete, along with five or six young men who have assumed the cap, and six or seven boys, I would wash in the River Yi, enjoy the breeze among the rain altars, and return home singing." Confucius heaves a sigh and shows his approval to Zeng Xi, saying, "I am with Dian." But Confucius' sense of mission kept him busy throughout his life.

*The Analects* initiated the style of employing quotations, which had a long-term influence upon later writings. The language of *The Analects* is close to colloquialism. What is recorded in the book is mainly brief expositions, both brilliant and full of genuine feeling. These are the strong points of writing by employing quotations. Quotations can also be found in later works such as *Mencius*, *Mozi* and *Zhuangzi*. By the time of the Song Dynasty, writings in the quotation style were further developed. Most Confucian scholars of the Song Dynasty made use of quotations in their writings. The most well-known works of quotations of the Song Dynasty include *Quotations from Cheng Hao and Cheng Yi* and *Quotations from Zhu Xi*.

The Confucian idea that "in education, there should be no distinction of social status," and of "teaching a person in accordance with his aptitude" have played a significant role in Chinese history. Emperor Kangxi of the Qing Dynasty inscribed the plaque of "Mentor and Icon of All Ages" for the Dacheng Palace Gate of the Beijing Confucian Temple, expressing great homage to the sacred philosopher and master.

# *Mencius*

Mencius (c. 372–289 BC), whose name was Ke, was a native of the State of Zou (southeast of the present-day Zouxian County, Shandong Province). He studied under a disciple of Zisi, grandson of Confucius. He not only carried on Confucius' thought but also further developed it. Deeply burdened with anxieties about the conditions of the age he lived in, and fearing that "The whole world is going crazy chasing after gains," Mencius started to spread the virtues of Yao and Shun of the remote past in glowing terms, appealing to everyone to take benevolence and righteousness as the foundation of the world. In the beginning, he set up a tutorial school at home and taught his disciples. Mencius said, "A gentleman's happiness lies in three things," and one of the three things is to "get from the whole kingdom the most talented individuals, and teach and nourish them." Later he toured various states and met with King Xuan of Qi and King Hui of Liang. Throughout the Warring States Period, "All the states contended for hegemony and encroachment upon each other through military forces." What the sovereigns of the time cared for most was nothing but political trickery. Consequently, it was impossible for the rulers of various states to adopt Mencius' doctrines, as it had been with Confucius. On the contrary, Mencius' views were considered to be "high-sounding and impractical." *Mencius* was partly written by Mencius himself and partly by his disciples with, by and large, the writing style of Mencius. The wording of the writings as a whole is forceful and the arguments are sharp and eloquent.

Mencius maintains that all people are good by nature and all people possess four beginnings. "The sense of compassion is the beginning of benevolence; the sense of shame the beginning of righteousness; the sense of modesty the beginning of decorum;

the sense of right and wrong the beginning of wisdom." Since all people are born good and have these four beginnings in themselves, the rulers only need to accord the people guidance so as to help them bring into full play the good in human nature instead of impeding it. "Men possess these four beginnings just as they possess their four limbs. Anyone possessing these four and saying that he can not do what is required of him is abasing himself." If people can have complete development of

A portrait of Mencius.

the good in their nature, they will be able to coexist in peace and harmony with their family, with other people and even with the whole of society.

If viewed from the perspective of prose writing, *Mencius* is different from the succinct style of *The Analects*. Though also written in the style of discourse, the writings in *Mencius* are at most times lengthy and the debates meticulously organized. Moreover, the style is stern and forceful, always teeming with the air of oratory. Mencius once said sarcastically, "How can you assume I am fond of debating? I do so because I have no alternative." In order to promote the practice of benevolent government, he reiterated his views in the debates with great patience. The opening part of "King Hui of Liang" of the first chapter of *Mencius* sets the tone of the whole chapter and even of the whole book. The first chapter starts with debates. Mencius goes to see King Hui of Liang, and the first thing King Hui of Liang asks is, "Venerable sir, since you have not counted it far to come here, a distance of a thousand *li*, may I presume that you are provided with counsels to profit my kingdom?" King Hui of Liang's most immediate concern is to inquire about what profit

Mencius has brought to him. The word "profit," in the mind of King Hui of Liang, refers in particular to the means that will help the State of Liang to become rich and powerful. Mencius, on the contrary, placing his stress on "benevolence and righteousness," replies, "Why must your Majesty use that word 'profit?' What I am provided with are counsels to benevolence and righteousness, and these are my only topics." Immediately after this, Mencius puts forth several parallel hypotheses. If King Hui of Liang concerns himself with "What is to be done to profit my kingdom?," the great officers will concern themselves with "What is to be done to profit our families?" and the inferior officers and the common people will concern themselves with "What is to be done to profit our persons?" If everyone only cares for the things which are of immediate concern or interest to him, "the superiors and the inferiors will probably try to snatch this profit from each other, and the kingdom will be endangered." Upon hearing King Hui of Liang's one-sentence inquiry about "profit," Mencius utters several sentences in succession in reply so as to advocate his doctrine of "benevolence and righteousness," which shows his efforts to talk the king into accepting his ideas through the rhetorical power of parallelism and running-on sentences. Apart from these rhetorical devices, Mencius also uses the method of discourse, quite similar to the wisdom of the Socratic method. Mencius' political stand is to "practice the benevolent government." He says, "One who uses force under the guise of benevolence will become the leader of the princes, but he must first be the ruler of a large state before he can do so. One who practices benevolence through the virtuous rule will become the unifier of the world, and to do so, his state need not be a large one. King Tang began to be such a ruler with a territory of only seventy *li*, and King Wen with one of a hundred." The core of Mencius' thought is "Of the first importance are the people, next comes the good of land and grains, and of the least importance is the ruler." In the

*Mencius' Mother Instructing Mencius*, by a Song artist. Legend has it that when Mencius was a child, his mother moved their home three times for the sake of his education. Under his mother's guidance and instruction, Mencius became a famous philosopher and educator in Chinese history.

context of his time, Mencius' thought was identified with a keen sense of democracy, but it would not be necessarily accepted by the rulers of the ducal states. After having given an account of his ideal "benevolent government," he sharply denounced the severe consequences resulting from "government by force" which was then practiced in every state, and it was not until King Hui of Liang said to Mencius, "I would like to seek your advice," that they started their conversation:

*Mencius said, "Is there any difference between killing a man with a club and with a sword?"*

**"Those who retreat fifty paces mock those who retreat a hundred"** appears in "King Hui of Liang (Part A)," *Mencius*, meaning that a person the same shortcoming or who has made the same mistake as others mocks those who have done so more seriously - a similar phrase to "the pot calling the kettle black."

**"Help the seedlings grow by pulling them upward"** appears in "Gongsun Chou (Part A)," *Mencius*, meaning that a person anxious to succeed goes against the laws of development, only to make things worse.

*The king said, "There is no difference."*

*"Is there any difference between killing a man with a sword and with bad government?"*

*"There is no difference," was the king's reply.*

*Mencius then said, "In your kitchen there is fat meat; in your stables there are strong horses. But your people look starved, and in the countryside are people dead from famine. That amounts to leading beasts out to devour men."*

Mencius once said, "He can not be led into dissipation by wealth and rank, nor deflected from his aim by poverty and obscurity, nor made to bend by power and force—all this is characteristic of a great man." In his writings, Mencius himself also appears to be such a great master. As he is sure that all men are born good, he is absolutely confident of his own innate nature, which can be seen from the lines, "A great man is one who keeps his heart as pure as a newborn baby's," "I'm strong in cultivating my vast vital energy," and "If, on introspection, I find myself in the right, I will press forward against even thousands of men."

Mencius is well-versed in drawing analogies. His writings are "Simple in diction but pregnant with meaning." Sayings like "Those who retreat fifty paces mock those who retreat a hundred" and "Help the seedlings grow by pulling them upward" have now become idioms known to every household.

# *Zhuangzi*

Zhuangzi (c. 369–286 BC) was Zhuang by family name and Zhou by given name. He was a scholar in the region of Meng in the State of Song (now somewhere near Shangqiu, Henan Province) during the mid-Warring States Period. When he was young, he once served as superintendent (a watchman) in a lacquer-yard. Zhuangzi was contemporary with King Hui of Liang and King Xuan of Qi. Little is known about the life of Zhuangzi except for some information given in *Records of the Historian* by Sima Qian. However, we can have a better understanding of his thought through his works. The extant book *Zhuangzi* consists of thirty-three chapters, which fall into three sections—"Inner Chapters," "Outer Chapters" and "Miscellaneous Chapters." It is generally acknowledged that the seven chapters contained in the "Inner Chapters" were written by Zhuangzi himself. Some of the thoughts conveyed in the "Outer Chapters" and "Miscellaneous Chapters" are also found to be identifiable to a certain extent with those conveyed in the "Inner Chapter." Taking advantage of this form of literature, Zhuangzi gives expression to the philosophical thought of Taoism. Owing to its unique ornate style and irregular and fantastic language, the book *Zhuangzi* appears to be more complicated, mystical and beautiful than the works of his contemporaries. For this reason, it is assumed that *Zhuangzi* marked the beginning of the school of "romanticism" in the tradition of Chinese literature. In addition, Zhuangzi's way of thinking about philosophical matters exerted a great influence on later generations. The Dark Learning (*Xuanxue*) of the Wei and Jin dynasties and the *Chan* sect of Buddhism in China can find their roots in *Zhuangzi*. Negligible as the influence of Zhuangzi's philosophy was upon political affairs, the role it played in modeling the personality of Chinese intellectuals was exceedingly significant. Zhuangzi pursues absolute spiritual freedom and strongly affirms the ideal that "The perfect man cares

A portrait of Zhuangzi.

for no self; the holy man cares for no merit; the sage cares for no fame." His writings are marked by boundless spiritual ethos and tremendous spiritual power.

Zhuangzi's prose shows us an incomparably spacious place. It reads:

*In the North Sea there is a kind of fish by the name of kun, whose size covers thousands of li. The fish metamorphoses into a kind of bird by the name of peng, whose back covers thousands of li. When if rises in flight, its wings are like clouds that hang from the sky. When the wind blows over the sea, the peng moves to the South Sea, the Celestial Pond.*

The fish the size of thousands of *li* — *kun* — metamorphoses into a kind of bird by the name of *peng* and, when it rises in flight, its wings are like clouds that hang from the sky. The spiritual ethos Zhuangzi aspires to is like the big flying bird, roaming freely in a space beyond the mundane world and "only seeking communication with the infinity of the heaven and the earth and showing no disdain for anything in the world." In terms of physical form, Zhuangzi takes after the holy man living on the faraway Mount Guye— "With his skin as white as ice and snow, he is as amiable as a virgin. He rides on the cloud, harnesses the flying dragon and roams beyond the four seas. By concentrating his spiritual power, he protects the creatures from the plague and ensures a bumper harvest." In addition to this, there are also some similarities between him and the recluses like Nanguo Ziqi who "sat leaning on his low table, gazed at the sky and breathed gently." Having abandoned the extreme self, Zhuangzi, though like a withered tree in appearance, hears the music of the heaven. When commenting on those who become slaves to worldly considerations, he says:

*Men of great wits are open and broad-minded; men of small wits are mean and meticulous. Men of great eloquence speak with arrogance; men of small eloquence speak without a point. They are restless when they are asleep and they are listless when they are awake. They are always involved in the outside world, daily embroiled in the battle of wits.*

Out of consideration for the true meaning of life, Zhuangzi regained his acute senses. So he could look into the minute details and the smallest subtleties of all the matters in the world and know both the imposing grandness and the trifling movements of all the things in the universe. Zhuangzi's writings are unusually imaginative. If we can say that people living in the age of *The Book of Songs* were much concerned with their own lives and the things closely related to them—"utilitarianism" — as we have mentioned previously in the chapter on *The Book of Songs*, and this "utilitarianism" could find its source in nature, then nature in Zhuangzi's writings was not used in the "material" sense of the word, but in the "spiritual" sense.

Zhuangzi's writings about the things in the world are usually allegorical, and his portrayal of nature precise. He wrote about birds, beasts, insects, fish, tortoises, and trees, as well as wind, clouds, mountains, and water. His description of minute, vivid details of the various sounds of wind in particular is fascinating:

*The universe blows out a vital breath called the wind. Sometimes it remains inactive, but once it becomes active, angry howls are emitted*

*Zhuangzi*, Guangxu years, Qing Dynasty

*from ten thousand crevices. Have you ever heard them roaring? There
are crags and cliffs in the mountains; there are hollows and caves in
the huge trees. They look like nostrils, mouths and ears, like gouges,
cups and mortars, and like pools and puddles. The wind blowing past
them makes sounds of the roaring water, whistling arrows, scolding,
breathing, shouting, wailing, rumbling, and chirping. One rustling
sound is echoed by another. A gentle breeze produces a faint response;
a strong wind produces a gigantic response. When the violent gust has
passed on, all the hollows become silent again.*

This is a passage from *On the Uniformity of All Things*. In this
passage, Nanguo Ziqi, the one who "sat leaning on his low
table," talks about the "three kinds of music" — "the music of the
earth, the music of the man and the music of the heaven" — by
making use of the various sounds produced from the hollows
and caves in the huge trees in the mountains. This passage is
originally targeted at explaining the uniformity of all things.
But if viewed from the perspective of "literary imagination," it
will not be difficult for us to realize that the author's description
of the various shapes of the trees and the sounds produced by
these hollows and caves are not only the result of the author's
careful observations, but also a projection of his powerful
imagination. In the light of this, the book *Zhuangzi*, though few
of the characters, things and places described in it are based on
fact, is considered the greatest of all the prose writings produced
during the period from the Pre-Qin times to the early Han
Dynasty.

Zhuangzi's thinking is unconventional. In his writings, many
eccentric and abnormal men with certain deformities are "holy
men," men who have attained enlightenment or immortality
through practicing Taoism. Apart from portraying Nanguo Ziqi,
a holy man who "sucks the wind, drinks the dew," he appears
to be most interested in artisans — people who possess special
skills. In the mind of Zhuangzi, these artisans are the ones who

are the nearest in distance to "Tao." These artisans are a butcher who carves a bullock, Artisan Shi who "waved his axe with a whirl and chopped off the speck of plaster which was as thin as a fly's wing from the Ying man's nose without hurting the nose," the hunch-backed old man with a concentrated mind. Zhuangzi's thought as conveyed in his works is always beyond expectations. In his writings, an empty skull can speak and a deformed man may well be the one who is the nearest in distance to "Tao." Zhuangzi himself even "sings and beats time on a basin" cheerfully at the death of his wife, saying that his deceased wife has returned to nature and "is now lying peacefully between the heaven and the earth."

Nevertheless, Zhuangzi also values life very much. Living in troubled times, he too was fully aware of how to protect his life effectively so as not to court his own destruction. Instead

*North Sea*, by Zhou Chen of the Ming Dynasty, depicts the great billows and waves of the ancient North Sea.

of giving a truthful account of what was going on in his mind, he made copious use of allegories in his writings. Zhuangzi designated Hui Shi in his writings as a strong counterpart in debate. In most cases, Hui Shi appeared as the opposites of Zhuangzi's viewpoints. The following famous allegory about a phoenix and an owl may serve as an example.

The phoenix was a holy bird living in the south. It set out from the South Sea and flew toward the North Sea. "It stopped only on the parasol tree, ate only the bamboo fruit and drank only the sweet water from the spring." As it passed by, an owl which had just caught a rotten rat looked up and threatened with a screech, reckoning that the phoenix had come to grab its rotten rat.

This is a very famous passage from "Autumn Floods" in *Zhuangzi*. Zhuangzi told Hui Shi this story to express his contempt for position and power. During the time when Hui Shi

*Dreaming of Butterflies*, by Liu Guandao of the Yuan Dynasty. This painting refers to the story that Zhuangzi once dreamed of being a butterfly. It exhibits Zhuangzi's philosophy of the equality of all beings.

became the prime minister of King Hui of Liang in the State of Wei—the same King Hui of Liang whom Mencius had visited—someone told Hui Shi that Zhuangzi had come to the State of Wei wishing to replace him as the prime minister. Thereupon, Hui Shi grew afraid and sent people to search for Zhuangzi for three days and three nights. Later, Zhuangzi went and saw Hui Shi and told him this allegory, which expressed Zhuangzi's viewpoint of regarding the position of prime minister as a rotten rat. Obviously, the two were as far apart in aspiration and interest as heaven and earth. Aside from this, there are still many more famous allegories in *Zhuangzi*, such as "Dismember an ox as skillfully as a cook" and "An ugly woman imitates a famous beauty knitting her brows."

**"Dismember an ox as skillfully as a cook"** appears in "Essentials for Keeping Good Health," *Zhuangzi*. Once upon a time, a cook dismembered an ox with superb skills for King Hui of Liang. The cook's knife moved freely and rhythmically between and along the bones without any obstacles. King Hui of Liang commended the cook's excellent skills. The cook said that he had been dismembering oxen for nineteen years and was very familiar with the physiological structure of the ox. This saying means that with practice one can learn to do things with skill.

**"An ugly woman imitates a famous beauty frowning"** appears in "The Movements of the Heaven," *Zhuangzi*. Xishi was a beauty of the State of Yue during the Warring States Period. One day she had a pain and felt unwell so she had a frown on her face when she went out. An ugly girl who lived nearby saw her and thought she looked very beautiful. So she imitated Xishi, but produced a ludicrous effect. Later generations called this ugly girl Dongshi. The saying "an ugly woman imitates a famous beauty frowning" suggests blind imitation with ludicrous effect.

# Qu Yuan

## A Romantic Lyricist

# Qu Yuan

By the time of the Warring States Period (475–221 BC), Qu Yuan, the first great poet of China, emerged. Qu Yuan was born in the State of Chu around the year 343 BC (or 353 BC), not long after the birth of Mencius and Zhuangzi. During the period of time prior to the Han Dynasty (206 BC–AD 220), there were actually no writers who took "literary creation" as an occupation. As a matter of fact, Qu Yuan was a statesman,

A portrait of Qu Yuan.

but he wrote over twenty poems, among which *The Lament on Encountering Sorrows* (also known as *Li Sao*) and *Asking Heaven* (*Tian Wen*) are poems as long as several hundred lines, having an extensive coverage ranging from all the things between the heaven and the earth to worldly affairs and current politics. Qu Yuan is generally acknowledged as the founder of the elegies of the State of Chu. His followers include Song Yu and some others. Elegies of Chu "were written in the Chu language, chanted with Chu pronunciation, and described places and objects in Chu." In other words, the elegies of Chu are poems with strong local characteristics. They were not only written in the dialect of the State of Chu, but also could be chanted to the music of the State of Chu. As a matter of fact, some of the words used in the elegies of Chu were also in common use nationwide before and during Qu Yuan's time. The character "xi" ("兮") in particular, which is a prominent feature of the elegies of Chu, had already been in use in the "Court Hymns," ("Ya") "Sacrificial Songs" ("Song") and "Folk Songs" ("Guofeng") of *The Book of Songs*.

When we say Qu Yuan was the founder of the elegies of Chu, we mean Qu Yuan made further developments and did recreations on the basis of summarizing the Chu folksongs. Qu Yuan "had both wide learning and a retentive memory, had an insight into political situation, and was gifted with a silver tongue." But his life was full of frustrations. He used to hold high official posts in the State of Chu and was for a time unquestionably trusted by King Huai of Chu. Later, "his faithfulness led to calumniation," and he "was repulsed with anger by the king of Chu." In the end, he committed suicide by throwing himself into the river. During the Warring States Period in which Qu Yuan lived, various ducal states began to take shape in succession with the decline of the Zhou Dynasty. The State of Qin and the State of Chu were the strongest rivals of the time. Qu Yuan regarded Qin as the "kingdom of tigers and wolves, a threat to Chu." But this insight made pro-Qin senior Chu officials look on him as a thorn in their flesh. For this reason, Qu Yuan was calumniated many times and was finally reviled by the king of Chu, which eventually resulted in Qu Yuan's departure from the capital of Chu. Consequently, Qu Yuan "wrote *The Lament on Encountering Sorrows* from rumination over the fate of his country." At the critical moment when Chu was being attacked by Qin, Qu Yuan returned to the capital of Chu and was sent to the State of Qi to ask for reinforcements. He succeeded in calling in reinforcements and rescuing Chu from the siege. Upon returning to Chu, he was appointed as the Lord of the Three (Family Lane) Portals, conducted the grand ceremony of calling back the spirit of tens of thousands of soldiers and generals who had laid down their heroic lives in the Qin-Chu battle and wrote the poem "Requiem." When the State of Qin and the State of Chu became related through marriage, Prince Zilan, the youngest son of King Huai of Chu, on the pretext of "How can we sever our friendly ties with Qin?" strongly insisted that King Huai of Chu go and visit Qin as the king of Qin had requested of him. But Qu Yuan was firmly against King Huai of Chu's going to Qin. In the end King Huai of Chu was imprisoned after he arrived at the Qin court and he later died there. In the years that followed, Qin troops massed threateningly on the border of Chu. Under such circumstances, Qu Yuan talked abusively of Zilan's unwise move and this offended Zilan. The one who succeeded to the throne was King Qingxiang, elder brother of Prince Zilan. Acting on Zilan's instigation, courtier Shangguan brought false charges against Qu Yuan, which proved effective. This time, Qu Yuan was banished from the land. During the many years of his exile, he always entertained some expectations of Chu. But by the year 278 BC, Qin troops had captured the capital of Chu. Then they pressed on southward step by step until finally they closed in on the locality of Qu Yuan's exile in 277 BC. Wading across the rivers and the water, Qu Yuan retreated time and again until he finally

*Asking Heaven*, by Liu Lingcang.

reached the Miluo River, which was located to the northeast of the Yangtze River. At that time, the State of Chu was as good as lost. Unwilling to be captured and losing all hope in Chu, Qu Yuan, in grief and indignation, committed suicide by throwing himself into the Miluo River. The Chu people cried out against the injustice done to Qu Yuan and deeply sympathized with his bitter experience. The date Qu Yuan drowned himself fell on the fifth day of the fifth lunar month. To commemorate his death, people held dragon-boat competitions on this day every year, and at the same time made *zongzi* and threw them into the river so that the wronged soul of Qu Yuan could eat. With the passing of time, the fifth day of the fifth month became the Duanwu Festival—a festival celebrated by all Chinese people.

Qu Yuan was the first great poet in Chinese history. His patriotism and his spiritual isolation is represented by the line "The crowd is drunk, I alone am sober." His perseverance in the pursuit of truth have had a far-reaching influence on Chinese intellectuals of later generations.

## The Lament on Encountering Sorrows

In terms of literary genre, no established names were given to Qu Yuan's works in general at the time when he wrote them. By the time of the Western Han Dynasty, Qu Yuan's works, as well as those by his followers, were given the standard name "Elegies of the State of Chu," first by Sima Qian and then by Liu Xiang. First taking shape during the Warring States Period, when prose was greatly influenced by the free, bold and unrestrained style of writing prevalent at that time, the elegies of Chu broke through the bounds of brevity and repetitiveness established by *The Book of Songs*. The elegies of Chu, flooded with close questioning or introspection, were marked by diversity of sentence patterns and tension between the lines. Accordingly, the elegies of Chu often appeared to be more magnificent and spectacular in scale. The character "xi" ("兮") was a common word in *The Book of Songs* and most of the lines observed the same "four-character" sentence structure. But the sentence structures in the elegies of Chu were diversified and more flexible, with some lines each containing five or more characters. Poets of the elegies of Chu were not willing to stick fast to the form of four-character line, but other forms of writing had not yet taken shape. Subsequently, the character "xi" was used by the poets of Chu for rhythm's sake. The most frequently used rhythm in the elegies of Chu was "three-character + three-character + xi, three-character + three-character," which can be exemplified by the line aforementioned— "Heaving a sigh prolonged and wiping off my tears, / I grieve the life of our people with thorns and hardships laid."

Qu Yuan was a prolific poet. *The Lament on Encountering Sorrows* (also known as *Li Sao*) is the most important of all his works, as well as one of the masterpiece poems in Chinese literature. It is a long lyric poem and comprises 372 lines. Literally, "Li" means "suffering or undergoing or encountering" and "Sao" means "sorrows or throes." So "Li Sao" can be rendered into *The Lament on Encountering Sorrows.* The poem gives a vivid portrayal of the speaker, a man of a noble origin with a pure and noble character, who expresses his pent-up feelings. The first line of the poem is "A scion far of Emperor Gaoyang I am." Emperor Gaoyang was the grandson of Huangdi, the common ancestor of all the Chinese people. From

A painted *Dou* Pot excavated from the Chu tombs of the Warring State Period, Hubei Province, representing the free, romantic and mysterious culture of the State of Chu.

this we can see the nobleness of the blood lineage of the poet or the speaker "I." "At morn, I drink the magnolia's dripping dews, / At nightfall, I on asters' fallen petals dine." What the poet drinks and has for food are dews from magnolia and fallen petals from asters, both of which are symbols of nobleness and purity. But the age the poet belongs to is one in which "I see those junta men all take to pleasures ill, / Their paths are dark and hazardous," and "The rabble, greedy for gains and power, rushes on, / Chock-full, yet still not content with what it has got; / Each of them, self-condoning and doubting others, / Becomes bristling with envy rancid and hot." The common practice of these men is "Truly to craft alone their praise they pay, / The square in measuring they disobey; / The use of common rules they hold debased; / With confidence their crooked lines they trace." In these lines, "those junta men" and "the rabble" are aimed at the aristocrats and their offspring who are in power and shameless greedy. When referring to the people of the lower strata of society who have neither power nor position, the poet uses the word "people." The line "Heaving a sigh prolonged and wiping off my tears, / I grieve the life of our people with thorns and hardships laid,"—one of the most famous lines in Qu Yuan's poems—voices the poet's deep grief and concern for the national crisis of the State of Chu and the disastrous situation of the common people.

In *The Lament on Encountering Sorrows*, Qu Yuan gives some thought on several roads that he might possibly take and his deliberation on the various roads is manifested in the form of discourse between several persons. His elder sister exhorts him tirelessly: since his concern for his country and people would not be appreciated, why should he continue like this and hold himself aloof with a stubborn will, only to get rejected by others? But Qu Yuan was bent on his own will and forged straight ahead. "Bending my nature and restraining my will, / I chew the cud of blame and the disgrace gulp down." He would know no regret at all even if he "stands on spotlessness and dies an upright death." During his exile, he asked a shaman to show forth his future. The shaman said, trying to talk him into leaving his native country, "What place is there where orchids flower not fair? / Why is thy native land thy single care?" But Qu Yuan, as a noble of the State of Chu and feeling greatly honored to have the family name of Qu, one of the three major family names in Chu, hated to leave. The lines "My way lies remote and so far, far away; / I shall go up and down to make my long search," were the standards he set for himself at the time, but the end of the long way, as it turned out later, was death.

Qu Yuan's poems were beautifully written. In addition, he was also the first poet who likened aromatic herbs and autumnal eupatories to his own and others' personalities and used plants to symbolize, people's character and moral integrity. On the other hand, the cardinal properties of the elegies of Chu were also unyielding, forceful and vigorous. These

*The Ladies of Xiang River*, by Wen Zhengming of the Ming Dynasty, collection of the Palace Museum, Beijing.

cardinal properties were grounded on the poet's concern for his country and people and supported by his upright character and perseverance in pursuit of truth. In the opening lines of *The Lament on Encountering Sorrows*, the poet's image appears before our eyes as a man of passion, wearing aromatic herbs on the shoulders and autumnal eupatories as a pendant: "Endued thus with selineas and angelicas, / I wear as pendant ruffle eupatories autumnal." Qu Yuan once held the official post of the "Lord of the Three (Family Lane) Portals," taking charge of the family affairs of the three royal families, Zhao, Qu and Jing, and at the same time being responsible for the education of the children from these three families. He wrote in *The Lament on Encountering Sorrows* thus:

*I've planted nine fields of eupatories sweet, / And raised a hundred mu of fragrant coumarous, / Together with fifty acres of azalea bright, / And asarums and angelicas fresh and new. / Expecting sore their foliage would then flourish fast, / I wish I could in due time reap an odorous crop.*

Here, Qu Yuan has an image of a gardener. He planted sweet flowers and beautiful grasses like fragrant coumarous and likened the children from the three royal families to asarums and angelicas fresh and new. Placing great hopes on them, he expected they would be able to display their talent and do well in life when they grew up. But, as it turned out later, Qu Yuan lost all hopes in them:

*Eupatory and angelica spread sweets naught, / Acorus and coumarou have changed into reeds. / Why is the odorous herbage of yesterdays / Turned directly into artemesias today?*

For this reason, Qu Yuan said, "I do grieve the scentful herbage rot and drop!"

Images of beauties also appeared frequently in Qu Yuan's poems and most of them were used metaphorically. However, interpretations of the images of beauties have been different throughout the ages. Some held that Qu Yuan likened the beauty to himself and likened the monarch to the image of a husband, and that the relationship between the monarch and the minister was like that of husband and wife, while some others held that sometimes the beauty referred to Qu Yuan himself and sometimes referred to the king of Chu:

*As days and months away do haste without a pause, / So spring and autumn alternate by turns always; / Reflecting on the trees and herbage falling sear, / I fear the Beauteous One would grow old too someday.*

Comparing himself to the "Beauteous One" whose charms would soon fade, Qu Yuan was seized with anxieties that the king of Chu would no longer put him to any use. If viewed from the perspective of likening the "Beauteous One" to the king of Chu, Qu Yuan was worried that the king of Chu would accomplish nothing before he got old.

Qu Yuan's elegies of Chu and *The Book of Songs* differ both in form and poetic thought. Poems in *The Book of Songs* are imbued with primitiveness and naivety, while Qu Yuan's poems are in the main intense and passionate and heterogeneous in content and "more visionary in thought and more ornate in language." The style of *The Book of Songs* is "mild and sincere," whereas Qu Yuan's verse "comes directly from his heart and abides by no established rules" (*An Outline History of Chinese Literature*, by Lu Xun). This is why those who hold *The Book of Songs* as the orthodox source of Chinese poetry are often inclined to criticize

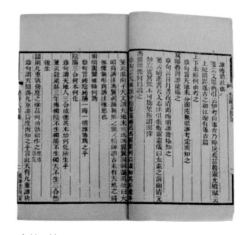

Asking Heaven.

criticisms at elegies of Chu. However, the influence the elegies of Chu have had upon Chinese literature is in fact greater than that of *The Book of Songs*. Qu Yuan lived in the Warring States Period, which saw the extensive flourishing of prose. The language of Qu Yuan's poetry received the baptism of prose writing, but he made efforts towards the direction of writing in verse. Practically every line of Qu Yuan's poems was rhymed and antitheses were widely used too, which mapped out the basics for later Chinese poetry. The four-character line with a two-character rhythm is the most prominent feature of almost all the poems in *The Book of Songs*. Qu Yuan's elegies of Chu initiated the form of three-character rhythm in poetry writing, which opened the road of the three-character rhythm for five- and seven-character poems and exerted an influence for more than a thousand years on Chinese poetry. Qu Yuan's poems are either "lucid, beautiful, and sorrowful," or "elaborate and melancholy," or "gorgeous

Qu Yuan Temple in his hometown of Zigui, Hubei Province.

and exotic, and resourceful," or "dazzling and full of inner beauty." "This is why elegies of the State of Chu surpasses past and contemporary works in spirit or excellence of language. Its brilliance and exquisite beauty are insurmountable" (Liu Xie: "Evaluating *The Elegies of the State of Chu*," *Dragon-carving and the Literary Mind*). The romanticism in the elegies of Chu can find its origin in *Zhuangzi*. Zhuangzi, however, maintaining that "people were lost to the pleasures of material wealth and could not be argued with or reasoned with," landed himself in nihilism. Contrary to Zhuangzi, Qu Yuan, though frustrated, was persevering in the pursuit of truth and even gave his own life for his ideals. Qu Yuan wrote his works with his life, his passion and his literary grace, and his poems "have their own lofty style." Chinese poets from the later centuries, like Li Bai and Su Shi, were the foremost followers of Qu Yuan.

**Liu Xie and his *Dragon-Carving and the Literary Mind***
Liu Xie (465–520) was a renowned literary theorist of the Southern and Northern dynasties. *Dragon-Carving and the Literary Mind* is in ten volumes and consists of fifty chapters that are divided into two parts with each part containing twenty-five chapters. The content of *Dragon-Carving and the Literary Mind* includes four major parts: general remarks, genre theory, literary creation theory and critical theory. *Dragon-Carving and the Literary Mind* established Liu Xie's important position in the history of Chinese literature and in the history of Chinese literary criticism.

# Records of the Historian

The First and Last Work by
Historians, *Li Sao* without Rhyme

# Pre-Qin Historical Books

The Chinese people started keeping records of history a long time ago. Court historians, whose job was to record current events, had already emerged during the Shang Dynasty (1600–1046 BC). The *Collection of Ancient Texts* (*Shangshu*) is the earliest collection of historical documents. Though the question of the precise time when the book was written is still open, it is beyond any doubt that the book existed in the early years of the Zhou Dynasty (c. eleventh century BC). The book *Collection of Ancient Texts*, consisting of twenty-eight chapters and arranged in chronological order, falls into four books. The first two are "The Book of Yu" and "The Book of Xia," and the following two "The Book of Shang" and "The Book of Zhou." Both historical events and official documents and official papers are included in *Collection of Ancient Texts*. But, relatively speaking, the book, simple and unadorned in style and archaic and abstruse in

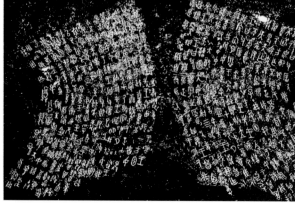

Mao Gong *Ding* Vessel, collection of the Palace Museum, Beijing. The inscriptions on this vessel meticulously record the Zhou Emperor's imperial mandate to Mao Gong. It can be regarded as a chapter of the *Collection of Ancient Texts* preserved on the vessel.

language, falls short of literary grace and excellence. The writing style of the *Collection of Ancient Texts* has had a limited influence on later literature. But the basic forms of writing typical of this book, namely deliberations at court, memorials to the throne, records of political events and policies, royal edicts and orders and orations, have exerted certain influence on the writing of official papers since the Han Dynasty. It is believed that the *Collection of Ancient Texts* is distinctive for putting official documents and texts on record. Of all the historical books, *The Spring and Autumn Annals* is the one that gives the most prominence to recording events. Originally, the "Spring and Autumn Annals" was a general term for the chronicles written by the official historians from each individual state during the Zhou Dynasty. *The Spring and Autumn Annals* of the State of Lu was actually co-authored by official historians from the State of Lu in different periods. Later Confucius revised it. Today when we talk about *The Spring and Autumn Annals,* we refer in particular to the annals of the State of Lu which had been revised by Confucius. It was the first dynastic history book written with annalistic style in China. *The Spring and Autumn Annals* gives priority to the historical events of the State of Lu, but the other co-existing states are also involved. It not only gives an account of the history of the State of Lu, but also brings to light the interrelationship between different historical facts in the same period, exhibiting a broad vision and all-inclusive magnificence. Deeply concerned by the moral degeneration of the time, Confucius used the historical book *The Spring and Autumn Annals* of the State of Lu to "praise virtue and censure vice" and make "traitors and evildoers in the world tremble with fear and awe" so as to attain the goal of preserving the rites of Zhou and ultimately bringing order out of chaos. For this reason, the wording in *The Spring and Autumn Annals* is both precise and implicit. Sometimes just one word of comment can give expression to the author's points of view towards the personage. This writing style of "using pithy remarks to convey deep meaning" was followed by men of letters in later generations and people named it "subtle words with a profound message."

Commentary books on *The Spring and Autumn Annals* are numerous, but *Zuo's Commentary*, which was allegedly said to have been written by Zuoqiu Ming of the Spring and Autumn Period, has enjoyed a good reputation. *Zuo's Commentary* excels in recounting historical events: "when describing triumphs, all the gains and rewards come into sight; when relating defeats, we see the collapse of routed troops; when narrating taking oaths of alliance, fervor is graphically reflected; when depicting craftiness, cheating and false charges are visible; when coming to favors, we feel the warmth of the spring sunshine; when coming to severity, we feel bitingly cold; when telling about the rise and prosperity of the country, boundless jubilation and cheers overflow; when stating the fall of the state, massive bleakness and compassion abound." (from "Part One, Miscellaneous," *Understanding History* by Liu Zhiji) *Zuo's Commentary* recounts as many as three to four hundred battles, sometimes describing calmness in devising strategies within a command tent and sometimes depicting the fierceness of the shining spears and armored horses, but at most times attaching greater importance to the former, which highlights pre-war preparations and strategy planning. This style of writing exerted a great influence on writing about warfare in Chinese literary works produced in the following thousand years.

# About *Records of the Historian*

The best-known historical book in China after *Zuo's Commentary* is *Records of the Historian*, the first general history in China written in the form of a series of biographies. *Records of the Historian* was written by Sima Qian of the Western Han Dynasty

(c. 145–c. 86 BC). *Records of the Historian* covers all developments in the fields of politics, economy and culture over three thousand years starting with the legendary Huangdi (Yellow Emperor), down to Emperor Wu of the Western Han Dynasty. It created five forms of historical writings, including emperors' biographies (basic annals), memorials to the emperors

A portrait of Sima Qian.

(tables), treatises, hereditary houses of nobles and princes, and biographies of historical figures. Among these five forms, the emperors' biographies, hereditary houses of nobles and princes and biographies of historical figures have had an extraordinarily far-reaching influence upon Chinese literature of later ages.

Sima Qian started to learn classics at an early age. For some time he studied *The Spring and Autumn Annals* under the guidance of Dong Zhongshu, a great Confucian classicist of the time. When he reached the age of twenty, he traveled widely, investigating the ruins of Emperor Yao and Emperor Shun in the south and experiencing the tradition of Confucianism in the former states of Qi and Lu in the north. All this laid the foundation for the writing of *Records of the Historian* in the days to come. His father, Sima Tan, who used to be the imperial historian, once made up his mind to write a historical book. After his father's death, Sima Qian, at the age of thirty-eight, succeeded his father as grand historian and carried forward his father's unfinished wish, and began to collect historical materials for his history. At forty-two, he started to write *Records of the Historian*. He was then punished by Emperor Wu of Han with castration for his defense of General Li Ling who surrendered to the Huns. After he was set free from prison, he was appointed palace secretary. Humiliated and distressed, he nevertheless went on writing the history and finally completed the work. In addition to this, through the writing of *Records of the Historian*, he also developed his idea that most writings were "emotional outlets for the pent-up feelings of the sages."

*King Wen of Zhou, when earl of the West, was in captivity and elaborated the Book of Changes; Confucius was in a desperate situation and wrote The Spring and Autumn Annals; Qu Yuan was banished, and only then composed the Li Sao; Zuoqiu Ming lost his sight, and he wrote The Discourses of the Domains; Sun Bin had his feet amputated, and then his The Art of War was drawn up; ...The Book of Songs. All these were for the most part written as the emotional outlets for the pent-up feelings of the sages. All of these men had something eating away at their hearts; they could not carry through their ideas of the Way, so they gave an account of what had happened before while thinking of those to come.*

Sima Qian held that because all the authors of the great classics in ancient China, such as the *Book of Changes, The Spring and Autumn Annals, Li Sao,* and *The Book of Songs* and so on, had something eating away at their hearts after they fell into desperation, they took to writing to give vent to their pent-up feelings. Actually the same can be said of Sima Qian. *Records of the Historian* has been acclaimed as a "faithful record" for its containing "no praises undeserved and no demerits covered up." Later comments on Sima Qian led to the conclusion that *Records of the Historian* was written "strictly in line with historical facts." However, it was too difficult a task to keep records of history "strictly in line with historical facts." "Faithful record" or "faithful account" in the strict sense often requires a historian to pass no judgment on the rights and wrongs. On the contrary, Sima Qian was often inclined to give expression in a straightforward manner to his judgments on morality and his orientations in

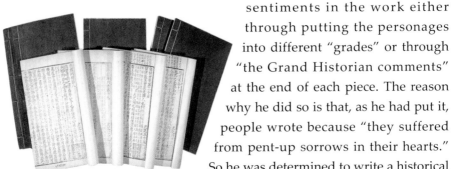

*Records of the Historian.*

sentiments in the work either through putting the personages into different "grades" or through "the Grand Historian comments" at the end of each piece. The reason why he did so is that, as he had put it, people wrote because "they suffered from pent-up sorrows in their hearts." So he was determined to write a historical book that "fully explores the interaction between Heaven and Man and gives a complete and authoritative account of the historical changes of the past and present." He had both the courage and motive to challenge the values prevalent at the time and develop an independent discourse that was entirely of his own. He criticized the emperor of his own time in "The Treatise on the Balanced Standard" and denounced current evil practice in "The Harsh Officials." In "The Money-Makers" he voiced his disagreement with the practice of valuing agriculture more highly than commerce.

# Characterization in *Records of the Historian*

The influence *Records of the Historian* exerted upon literature of later ages is manifold. The most significant influence perhaps lies in its portrayal of characters. Xiang Yu was a tragic hero who rose in arms in the region of Chu during the last years of Qin and later contended for the rule of the country and eventually cut his throat when routed. Though Xiang Yu was active for only eight years in the historical time and space of Qin and Han, "Xiang Yu" in *Records of the Historian* gives an incisive and vivid depiction of this hero whose strength "uprooted mountains and whose spirit overtopped the world," covering his irresistible valor in taking cities and seizing territories, his majestic appearance when staring angrily at people and uttering denouncements on the battlefields, and his deep attachment to his concubine Lady Yu and his steed, as well as his tragic death caused by his refusal to cross the river. However, Sima Qian did not steer clear of Xiang Yu's various weaknesses and defects in his writings. He criticized Xiang Yu by saying, "He boasted of his conquests, trusted only his personal judgment and did not follow ancient precedents." Apart from this, he also commented that Xiang Yu was shortsighted, suspicious and jealous, brave but not resourceful, and ruthless and bloodthirsty. In "Xiang Yu," Sima Qian gave an account of Xiang Yu's evildoings of massacring more than two hundred thousand Qin soldiers who had laid down their arms, massacring the citizens of Xianyang and setting fire to the Qin palaces after he took the Qin

*The Banquet of Hong Men* is a story from "Xiang Yu," *Records of the Historian*. The feud of Chu and Han begins there and Sima Qian vividly captures the open and secret strife at the banquet.

capital. Moreover, various accounts of Xiang Yu's temperament were also given by the characters in the biographies of other personages. Some said that Xiang Yu "... is kind, generous and considerate... He is jealous of capable and virtuous people, and he murders officials who have performed outstanding service and distrusts men of virtue." Some commented that "When Xiang Yu bellows with rage a thousand men are rooted to the ground, but since he cannot appoint worthy commanders all he has is the courage of a single man. He is polite, kindly and an amiable talker. If a man falls ill he will shed tears and share his meal with him; but when a man renders such services that he deserves a fief, Xiang Yu plays with the seal till its corners are rubbed off before he can bring himself to part with it. This is what is called womanly kindness." Han Xin, chief marshal during Liu Bang's reign, made this comment on Xiang Yu. What he meant is that Xiang Yu "had the courage of a single man" and "womanly kindness" only in name and would not be able to accomplish anything great. Qian Zhongshu, a contemporary Chinese scholar, noticed the complexity of Xiang Yu's disposition as portrayed in *Records of Historian* and thus commented: "Amiable when talking" and "roaring with anger," "polite and kindly" and "intrepid and cunning," "kind and respectful to talented people" and "jealous of capable and virtuous people," "womanly kindness" and "bloodthirstiness," and "sharing his meal with others" and "refusing to give awards," all these dispositions of Xiang Yu are opposite and contradicting, but are at the same time unified in Xiang Yu alone, just like a person writing with both right and left hand or singing different tunes with one throat. In spite of this, the character of Xiang Yu still remains consistent. If viewed in the light of modern psychology, Xiang Yu's character is plausible.

Sometimes Xiang Yu spoke in a soft, low voice and was considerate, while sometimes he bellowed with rage and killed people like flies; sometimes he shared his meal with other men and even shed tears at the sight of others' suffering, but he appeared to be petty when he failed to give awards to those who had done meritorious service, which resulted in his loss of popular support. These different dispositions of Xiang Yu, opposite and contradicting, are not reflected concurrently in Sima Qian's writings. "Xiang Yu" concentrates on depicting the illustrious image of Xiang Yu as a peerless hero, while Xiang Yu's defects and weakness are described in the biographies of other personages through the "mutually explanatory and supplementary method." By doing so, the image of a tragic hero is established in "Xiang Yu." "Xiang Yu" starts when he was a boy. As a boy, Xiang Yu first studied to be a scribe and then took up swordsmanship, but failed in both. After this, he became interested in military strategy, but again he refused to study it to the end. It is thus clear that Xiang Yu was careless in character when he was still young. Nevertheless, when he happened to witness the ostentation and momentum of the First Emperor of Qin who was going on an inspection tour in the south, he exclaimed, "why not take over from him?" From this we see his ambition. After he rose in arms, his fame spread to other states after the battle of Julu. When Qin was defeated, Xiang Yu "struck terror into the hearts of all the armies from other states." When he summoned generals from the other states to his camp, "they entered on their knees and none dared to look up." This was possibly the zenith of Xiang Yu's fame and power. From then on, all the forces of these different states took orders from him. Later he led his troops west, took Xianyang and massacred the citizens there, set fire to the Qin palaces and thus put an end to the unified domain of the Qin regime. Later, he suffered defeat at the banquet held at Hongmen, at which an attempt was made on Liu Bang's life. He fell into the trap set up by Liu Bang to play his generals off against him and eventually was hemmed in on all sides by Liu Bang's troops at Gaixia. With solemn fervor, Xiang Yu chanted a tragic air, bid farewell to his favorite concubine, mounted his horse and broke through the enemy lines, killed enemy commanders and cut down their flags, and, after killing several dozens of enemy soldiers, killed himself by cutting his throat.

Deeply impressed by the speed of Xiang Yu's rise and fall, Sima Qian, in "Xiang Yu," gave a vivid description of Xiang Yu's authority and influence when he was at the height of his power, as well as his tragic but heroic death when he suffered the crushing defeat. "Xiang Yu," imbued with both sublime heroism and sentimental sadness, is probably the most remarkable biography in *Records of the Historian*. It represents Sima Qian's writing style and skill in terms of characterization.

Lü Zhi, empress of Liu Bang, the first emperor of the Han Dynasty, is notorious in Chinese history for her ruthlessness

*The Lord's Farewell to His Concubine*, a Peking Opera, takes its story from an historic event. Xiang Yu is stranded at Gaixia and besieged on all sides. He toasts to Concubine Yu for a last farewell, and they commit suicide together. This became a classic of Peking Opera.

and malignancy. Consort Qi was Empress Lü's rival in love. Empress Lü chopped off Consort Qi's hands and feet, blinded her by scooping out her eyes, impaired her hearing and made her deaf and dumb with poison, abandoned her to live in a toilet, and insulted her as the "Human Pig." Three of Liu Bang's sons were persecuted to death by Empress Lü. In order to arrogate all power to herself, she ordered that all of Liu Bang's sons and nephews must marry her relatives—the girls by the family name of Lü, which resulted in incestuous marriages. Resolute and steadfast in character, Empress Lü assisted Liu Bang in seizing state power. For around ten years after Liu Bang's death, she maintained social stability: "Though (Empress Lü) ruled as a woman from within doors, the empire was at peace, there were few punishments and few criminals; the peasants tilled the land diligently, and there was an abundance of food and clothing." As a historian, Sima Qian laid stress on Empress Lü's talent in handling political affairs and meritorious deeds in governing the country and regarded them as positive in the biography of Empress Lü. Furthermore, he also marked off Empress Lü's political talent and moral integrity. Sima Qian did so with Empress Lü, and he did so too with Lü's husband, Liu Bang. Liu Bang was a selfish, lecherous, vulgar, and deceitful man. But he unified the whole country and freed the common people from the turmoil of war for years running, and consequently the common people had time to recuperate and rehabilitate. This was a great service rendered by Liu Bang. These two aspects of Liu Bang's career are well manifested in *Records of the Historian*.

# History and Literature

In the 1980s, "New Historicism" sprang up in American universities. New Historicism holds that all historical texts correspond to literary imagination (Hyden White). New historicists profess that a historian is in the first place a story-teller, and the sensitivity of a historian lies in his or her ability to create a credible story out of a series of "facts." The ability to create a story refers to holding back and playing down some elements and enhancing and giving priority to others, through characterization, repetition of theme, change of tone and viewpoints, alternative writing tactics and so on, in short, through all the plot-weaving techniques we usually employ in fiction and drama writing.

Prior to the emergence of "New Historicism" in the West, history and literature were usually isolated from each other, with history focusing on the rational and truthful and literature on perception. In China, some people lay emphasis on history while some others lay emphasis on literature in the study of *Records of the Historian*. Han Yu of the Tang Dynasty took *Records of the Historian*, along with *Zhuangzi, Elegies of the State of Chu* by Qu Yuan and rhyme prose by Sima Xiangru as the model for creative writing. Ever since then, people have looked upon it as literature. We might have a better understanding of the literary merits of *Records of the Historian* as a historical text in the light of modern western theory. The literary merits of *Records of the Historian*, in terms of writing techniques, lie in its vigorous and serene writing style. "Xiang Yu," as we have seen, may serve as an example of the writings typical of this style. As to the ornate and magnificent style or liveliness associated with literary writings, we can also pick them up in Zhuangzi's works. The literary merits of *Records of the Historian* lie primarily in the full expression of Sima Qian's subjective drive, in other words, the author, enduring the torture inflicted upon him by castration and filled with resentment, devoted himself to his own writing to such an extent that readers can feel as though they are experiences of their own: "I feel like ending my life when I read the biographies of gallant citizens; I feel like crying when I read 'Qu Yuan' and 'Jia Yi,' I feel like living in seclusion when I read 'Zhuangzi' and 'Lu Zhonglian,' I feel like rising in action immediately when I read 'Li Guang,' I feel like complying and being prudent when I read 'Shi Jian,' and I feel like keeping chivalrous men when I read 'Lord Xinling' and 'Lord Pingyuan'" (Mao Kun: *Letters on Works of Literature to Governor Cai Baishi*).

Sima Qian showed profound sympathy and understanding for talented men who had a life beset with trouble like Qu Yuan and Xiang Yu, as well as for gallant citizens and assassins. But he was by no means a man with narrow vision, like a frog at the bottom of a well. Owing to his extensive travels at an early age, his family background and his ambitions, he concerned himself with ordinary people across the land. *Records of the Historian* involves a great variety of fields. "The Treatise on the Balanced Standard," "The Treatise on Sacrificial Address to Heaven and Earth" and "The Money-Makers" touch upon economic and political issues. "The Treatise on the Balanced Standard" has long been regarded as a censure on the economic policies implemented by Emperor Wu of Han, under whose reign the once substantial national treasury began to show an aggregate deficit. Emperor Wu of Han not only hankered after material comforts and luxury, building palaces and making inspection tours around various prefectures, he also craved grandeur and success. He spent enormous amounts of money on military ventures and the construction of water works as well as famine and disaster relief. Aside from these efforts, unscrupulous merchants and wealthy people, regardless of the national interest, made profits by hoarding and speculating. All this resulted in national economic depression during the reign of Emperor Wu of Han. Nevertheless, Sima Qian also noticed the positive aspect of Emperor Wu's implementation of the "balanced standard" policy - regulating and controlling commodity prices. On the one hand, it cracked down on the monopolization of wealth and materials

A figure-painting brick of the Han Dynasty vividly captures social scenes.

by the rich and unscrupulous merchants and, on the other hand, greatly increased the property of the imperial family. Meanwhile, it also increased the wealth of the whole country. Sima Qian, as a historian, assessed his character from the perspective of both the national interest and the interests of the ordinary people.

In his *Poetics*, Aristotle said, "Poetry, therefore, is a more philosophical and a higher thing than history: for poetry tends to express the universal, history the particular." In the historical works of Sima Qian, we can see that when he relates particular events, he always places them against the immense historical backdrop of the time. For instance, when expounding the economic policy of Emperor Wu of Han, he associates it with the economic situation since the founding of the Han Dynasty; when writing about emperors, generals and ministers, gallant citizens and assassins, Confucian scholars and men of letters, he sets each of them in a particular spiritual vein of his own. This is why *Records of the Historian* is believed to have the qualities of "poetry." Lu Xun, the greatest Chinese writer of the twentieth century, paid his tribute to Sima Qian's *Records of the Historian* thus, "The first and last great work by historians, *Li Sao* without rhyme" (Lu Xun: "Sima Xiangru and Sima Qian," *An Outline History of Chinese Literature*).

# Literature in the Wei and Jin Period

## Jian'an Literature and Tao Yuanming

In the history of China, the period starting from the last years of the Eastern Han Dynasty to the Wei, Jin, Northern and Southern dynasties was a period of great change in politics, economy and culture. Drastic social turmoil and frequent replacement of dynasties made the unified domain of the Western Han and Eastern Han dynasties fall apart. The rule of the Confucian classics declined and, breaking through the doctrines and norms of Confucian classics, the minds of scholars were liberated. Dark Learning, a metaphysical sect that tried to integrate Taoism and Confucian doctrines, flourished.

Deeply affected by the turmoil of society, the destitution of people's livelihood, brevity of life, and the unpredictability of prosperity and decline and honor and disgrace, men of letters started to go further in meditations on life, bringing about a resurgence in the popularity of Zhuangzi's thought. With all sorts of feelings welling up in the minds of scholars, the function of expressing emotions and aspirations in poetry was brought into full play during this period. Literature of the Jian'an Period was represented by the works of the "Three Caos" and the "Seven Talented Writers." "A look at the works of this time shows that they were full of feeling. In an age of war and turmoil, when the world was corrupt and the people were discontented, poets pondered deeply and wrote with a poignant pen. Their works were spirited and impassioned" (Liu Xie: "Literature and the Times" in *Dragon-Carving and the Literary Mind*). Later generations called the above-mentioned features "the vigorous and powerful style of Jian'an literature." After bidding

**"The Three Caos"**
"The Three Caos" were Cao Cao and his sons Cao Pi and Cao Zhi, the leaders of Jian'an literature.

**"Seven Talented Writers"**
This refers to seven writers during the Jian'an Period, including Kong Rong, Chen Lin, Wang Can, Xu Gan, Ruan Yu, Ying Chang, and Liu Zhen.

farewell to Jian'an literature, which disdained fame and wealth, advocated emotions and individual personality and pursued the beauty of passion and sadness, men of letters and aristocrats throughout the Western Jin and Eastern Jin dynasties were seized with anxiety though they lived in peace and comfort, and were often drawn into the vortex of political struggles. Being on tenterhooks all the time and fearing that misfortune might come to them at any moment, they gave expression to their tendency towards complying with the environment and staying safe. Some poets wrote about mountains and rivers to vent their feelings, healing their hearts and calming their nerves. While Dark Learning was in vogue, the thoughts of Laozi and Zhuangzi became increasingly popular for a time and all men of literary talent considered it the fashion to talk about Dark Learning. Influenced by the plain and delicate theories of Dark Learning, works of literature expounding the Dark Learning popular in the Wei and Jin dynasties became prevalent. Abstract

*Seven Sages of the Bamboo Grove,* a New Year picture of Yangliuqing, Tianjin, Qing Dynasty.

concepts like "non-action," "nameless," "wandering in absolute freedom," and "uniformity of all things" flooded these works of literature. Therefore, "the poems of the time are permeated with Laozi's philosophy; the works of rhyme-prose are like commentaries on *Zhuangzi*." Having gradually realized their own historic mission, some men of literary talent departed from dangerous politics and chose to live in seclusion with resentment as a silent protest against the current political power. This distinctive feature was typical of men of literary talent in the Wei and Jin period. The most famous of the time were the "Seven Sages of the Bamboo Grove," Ruan Ji, Ji Kang, Shan Tao, Liu Ling, Ruan Xian, Xiang Xiu, and Wang Rong. Unrestrained and unconventional, they often retreated to the bamboo groves, engaging themselves in playing music and drinking wine. Their poetry was often about their broadmindedness, the natural landscape and their life in seclusion. By carrying forward the tradition of Ruan Ji, Ji Kang, and the like, Tao Yuanming perfected the poems of woods and streams and opened up a new realm for landscape and pastoral poetry. For this reason, Tao Yuanming was acclaimed as the "forerunner of reclusive poets past and present."

Born into an official's family that had become impoverished and declined in social status, Tao Yuanming (365–427) was a native of Chaisang, Xunyang (present-day Jiujiang, Jiangxi Province). In his later years, he changed his name to Tao Qian. His great grandfather Tao Kan used to hold the official position of Minister of Defense. His grandfather and father also used to hold official positions like governors and county magistrates. By the time of Tao Yuanming, the Tao family declined. At eight, his father died. At twelve, his mother also died of illness. When he was still young, Tao Yuanming lived with Meng Jia, grandfather on his mother's side. Meng Jia was a man of literary talent of the time. "Meng Jia was discreet in manners but was

*The Home Coming of the Drunk Yuanming*, by Zhang Peng of the Ming Dynasty, represents the elegance of Tao Yuanming appreciating wine and chrysanthemums.

never conceited and arrogant in speech. He never knew capriciousness. He was deeply fond of drinking, but never became muddle-headed, no matter how much he drank. When he was beside himself with joy, he just acted as if there were no one else present." Tao Yuanming followed his grandfather's philosophy of life to a considerable extent when he was in society. Naturally, his personality and self-cultivation well displayed his grandfather's influence upon him. During the Western Jin and Eastern Jin dynasties when all scholars established *Zhuangzi* and *Laozi* as the sole authority and rejected the "Six Classics," Tao Yuanming not only studied *Laozi* and *Zhuangzi* like the rest of the scholar officials of the time had done, he also studied the "Six Classics," prose works, and historical works of the Confucian school as well as some unconventional books like *The Book of Mountains and Seas*. The trend of the time and the influence of his family made him absorb both Confucian thought and Taoism, and this resulted in his having two different kinds of tastes and interests—when young, his ambitions soared, but by nature he loved the mountains and hills.

Influenced by his family background and Confucian thought, Tao Yuanming had great ambitions when he was still young— "Beyond the Four Seas my ambitions soared, / To far lands I wanted to wing my way." But all the high official positions were held by those from the distinguished families of power and influence. Tao Yuanming did not take up an official career until he was twenty-nine years old. During the ten years that followed, he served as an official several times, but all were low-ranking positions like ceremonial official or military secretary. He not only had little chance to realize his ambitions to be of help to the people and society, he also had to lower and humiliate himself so as to move in official circles. Under such circumstances, he felt "there was much he scorned in disdain" and "it was more painful to do or say things that went against his conscience."

Meanwhile, under the influence of his grandfather and Taoism, Tao Yuanming developed a strong love of nature and admired the life of seclusion at an early age, as was expressed in one of his poems:

*For thirty years I lived a leisured life / And always kept aloof from worldly strife. / I take the poems and books as my pursuit / For a tranquil rural life without dispute.*

When imperial service was hard for him, he wrote in one poem, "On second thought, the best is rural life, / And so I'll keep away from worldly strife." So throughout the ten years of his official career, he had been in a dilemma, and in his heart he was at one time an official and at another a recluse.

At thirty-nine, Tao Yuanming wrote:

*The Confucian teaching rings without doubt: / It's Tao, not poverty, that man should care about. / As this teaching is not worth my toil, / I change my mind and start to turn to the soil.*

Seeing that his ideals could not be realized, he started to make a living by farming. As Confucian thought looked down upon doing manual labor, most scholars and officials during the Wei, Jin, Southern and Northern dynasties regarded it as a disgrace to do farm work. Later, Tao Yuanming served as a military counselor and a military secretary. His last official position was the magistrate of Pengze County, but he only held office in Pengze County for eighty days. His superior officer sent an assistant to his county, and his own subordinate asked him to put on ceremonial dress to welcome this man. "I can't bow to anyone just for the sake of five pecks of rice," he said. On the same day he resigned from office and returned home to the countryside, which was:

*Ten acres built with scattered houses square, / Beside the thatched huts eight or nine in all; / There elms and willows shade the hindmost eaves, / With peach and pear trees spread before the hall.*

Thus he put an end to his official career and returned to his farm to live in seclusion.

The following twenty years were the peak of his literary creation. His pastoral poetry was held in high esteem by later generations, and was even acclaimed as the "basic norms of poetry writing" in the Song Dynasty. Living in retirement amidst the beautiful rural scenery, "While picking asters 'neath the eastern fence, / My gaze upon the southern mountain rests," Tao Yuanming kept himself away from the crowds of officials and nobles and obtained freedom and peace of the soul. The farm, greatly beautified by Tao Yuanming in verse form, was turned into a spiritual haven in a troubled world. Since Tao Yuanming's poems were mainly on rural life, he is always considered a "pastoral poet." With his own life, Tao Yuanming put into practice the idealized state of living a life in seclusion and writing poetry. As Lun Xun once commented, after Tao Yuanming had experienced so many turbulences and witnessed excessive abuses of political power, he stopped complaining and, henceforth, his poems became gentle and tranquil.

The prosaic rural scenery, the ordinary country life and a tranquil state of mind were fully illustrated in his poems through simple language and a simple style of writing. Outspoken and straightforward, his poetry appeared to be an integral whole and had no traces of man-made embellishment, as if it had flowed out naturally and freely from the depth of his heart. Poem One of "Reading *The Book of Mountains and Seas*" reads:

*In early summer weeds and woodlands teem; / The trees about my house with green increase; / The birds are pleased to find a place of rest, / And we like them to enjoy my home in peace. / When ploughing or when sowing I have done / I think it best to read my books at last. / Deep carriage ruts have scarred the narrow lane / Where old friends' carriages have often passed. / Contentedly we talk and pour spring wine, / Or pick the vegetables I have grown. / Soon a light drizzle hurries from the east, / By humid breezes hither to us blown. / I read the legends of the ancient prince, / Glancing at pictured mounts or painted seas; / Thus tranquily I pass my worldly span; / Why should I not rest happy and at ease?*

The beauty of the natural sceneries is given full expression in his "farmer's language," for instance, "A distant village gleams beneath the sun, / While smoke from nearby huts hangs in the breeze." There are also vivid descriptions of the people's life in his poems, such as:

*In pleasant days autumn and of spring / Climbing the hills new poems we shall recite. / Passing the threshold one the other calls, / If some have wine, the others they invite. / When farm work calls each to his fields returns, / At leisure then we wish to meet again; / Wishing to meet we quickly don our clothes, / For endless laughter and discussion fain.*

As seemingly commonplace as these lines are, an idyllic life is graphically described. Having done away with all the elements that are wordy and slow-moving, the language of Tao Yuanming's poetry presents a clear and bright simplicity. Later generations thus commented on Tao Yuanming's poetry: "Though simple and unadorned in outward appearance, his poetry is

*The Fairyland of the Peach-Blossom Springs*, by Qiu Ying of the Ming Dynasty. The most famous essay of Tao Yuanming is *The Peach-Blossom Springs*. He creates an ideal place described as the Peach-Blossom Springs. People there enjoy their lives and are aloof from worldly affairs. Later the poets Wang Wei, Han Yu, and Liu Yuxi all wrote poems on this topic and expressed their social ideals.

gorgeous and ornate in style; though thin in appearance, his poetry is rounded and rich in substance."

Among Tao Yuanming's extant prose works and descriptive poetic prose, "The Peach-Blossom Springs" and "I Had Better Return" are the most famous pieces. "The Peach-Blossom Springs" actually bears features of fiction. In it, Tao Yuanming created an imaginary ideal world, in which we can perceive not only the unsophisticated simplicity of the ancient times to which the Confucians had aspired, but also traces of the social pattern of "a small state with a sparse population" advocated by Laozi. The following description of the rural scenes matches well with the artistic ambience of Tao Yuanming's idyllic poems:

*The place he had come to was level and spacious. There were houses and cottages arranged in a planned order; there were fine fields and beautiful pools; there were mulberry trees, bamboo groves, and many other kinds of trees as well; there were raised pathways round the fields; and he heard the sound of chickens and of dogs. Going to and fro in all this, and busied in working and planting, were people, both men and women. Their dress was not unlike that of people outside, but all of them, whether old people with white hair or children with their hair tied in a knot, all were happy and content with themselves.*

"I Had Better Return" was written at the time when Tao Yuanming had made up his mind to resign from office and live a life in seclusion. In the various forms of literary writing in ancient China, descriptive poetic prose was always written in ornate language. Contrary to this, the style of this descriptive poetic prose by Tao Yuanming was simple and refreshing. In the line "Lightly my boat was rowed and rowed, and gently my gown by the wind was up rolled," the poet imagines his light-heartedness and cheerfulness, free and unrestrained, when he returns homeward. The lines that extol the beauty of natural sceneries, such as "Occasionally I raised my head to look at the distant cloud, / which had no intention to float out of the mountain side. / Even birds knew to return to the woods when they were tired," and "Trees are thriving and vigorous, / While springs flow murmuring and look marvelous," give a vivid portrayal of the charm of nature.

Tao Yuanming led a simple life in his hometown Chaisang, doing farm work, drinking wine, and writing poems about country life. He lived in abject poverty and firmly kept his moral integrity and refused to re-enter officialdom even when he came under such straitened circumstances as "Often I go hungry on summer days, / And on winter nights sleep without blankets." With a clear conscience he departed from the world forever.

# Li Bai and Du Fu

## The Two Summits of Tang Poetry

# Li Bai—A Romantic Genius

The height of the Tang Dynasty was the golden age of Chinese poetry. The great romantic poet Li Bai (701–762) was the outstanding representative poet of the poetry circles of the High Tang period. Li Bai's poetry gave full display to the high-mindedness and splendor of Tang culture.

A portrait of Li Bai.

Li Bai had an exceedingly unusual talent in poetic writing. Du Fu (712–770), Li Bai's contemporary and fellow celebrated poet, commented on Li Bai:

*In the past there was a man unrestrained, / Whom a celestial poet was acclaimed. / The storm was startled when he took up his writing brush; / Ghosts and gods wept copious tears after his poems were finished.*

("Remembering Li Bai on a Spring Day")

Li Bai's poetic creations are impassioned, bold and unrestrained, and romantic. They have exerted a far-reaching influence upon later generations, and have long been loved by the Chinese people. His short poem "Thoughts on a Tranquil Night" is listed in children's primers:

*Before my bed a pool of light— / Can it be hoar-frost on the ground? / Looking up, I find the moon bright; / Bowing, in homesickness I'm drowned.*

Li Bai's personal experiences played an important role in the formation of his poetic style. When he was still a child, he used to read books and study Taoism in the mountains and woods of his hometown. Leaving home in his twenties, he started to tour China and his footprints covered more than half of the country.

Many of his poems on nature and landscapes have enjoyed great popularity. The following is an example:

*The sunlit Censer Peak exhales incense-like cloud; / Like an upended stream the cataract sounds loud. / Its torrent dashes down three thousand feet from high / As if the Silver River fell from the blue sky.*
("The Waterfall in Mount Lu Viewed from Afar")

Li Bai's poetic language is fresh and unaffected, lucid and lively. The metaphors and similes he employs in writing are vivid. "Its torrent dashes down three thousand feet from high, /As if the Silver River fell from the blue sky" is incredible hyperbole and imagination. As a true expression of the poet's eulogy and love of nature, this poem forms a coherent whole and contains profound thoughts and sentiments as well as a strong flavor.

*The Waterfall in Mount Lu*, by Gao Qipei of the Qing Dynasty.

Li Bai lived in the Kaiyuan and Tianbao periods of Tang Xuanzong's reign. The Kaiyuan Period (713–741) is known as the "Times of Peace and Prosperity of Kaiyuan" in Chinese history, during which the country was unified, social economy and culture were unprecedentedly thriving and prospering, and intellectuals were provided with more chances and better conditions to give full play to their talent. Accordingly, the lofty sentiments and enterprising spirit cherished by scholars like Li Bai were greatly aroused. By nature Li Bai was self-confident and unrestrained, free and uninhibited. In his early youth he was fond of reading unique books and writing descriptive poetic prose, which demonstrated some initial symptoms of his talent. In his boyhood he practiced swordsmanship and led the life of a chivalrous swordsman. In one of his poems he wrote:

*Unacquainted with the ways of the world I was when I came of age, / But I associated with men of courage and chivalry. / ... / Making a living in the glint and flash of the swords, / I'd rather kill evildoers in the human society.*

The poet's complacent and untrammeled attitude towards chivalrous deeds was clearly expressed in these lines, and this attitude was not in the least weakened in his later works. In some of his poems, such as "The Ballad of Gallants and Men of Outstanding Talent in Fufeng," Li Bai expressed his respect and admiration for the chivalrous men from ancient times who were men of their word, who eliminated the evil and made known the good, and who belittled the official position. Aside from this, these poems also gave expression at a deeper level to his longing to be a hero and counselor himself, which exactly revealed that he himself also had the unusual talent and the ambition to bring the turbulent times back to order.

A prominent feature of Li Bai's temperament was his deep sense of self-confidence and conceitedness. He was very interested in politics and thought that he possessed the practical ability requested of the virtuous and able ministers and prime ministers of ancient times. When the imperial court was plunged into internal turmoil, he expected to be put in an important position by the rulers so that he would be able to put down riots and manage state affairs by exercising his wisdom and talent. However, Li Bai did not get such a chance throughout his life. He had a frustrated official career. He was banished from the court twice and endured all kinds of trials and tribulations. Denied the opportunity to render service for the country, Li Bai suffered greatly. As a consequence, feelings of agonizing pains and indignation interwoven with yearnings and despair came out spontaneously under his writing brush. He wrote a number of poems like "Hard is the Way to Shu" and "Hard is the Way of the World." But in fact, these poems voiced the poet's frustrations when he failed to have a smooth official career and failed to realize his talent and ambition due to the abuse of power of treacherous sycophants. This was why he sighed, "Hard is the Way. It is harder than to climb the sky."

At the age of forty-two, Li Bai was summoned to the court by Emperor Tang Xuanzong to be made an official. At this he was carried away with excitement, thinking that the time to display his talent had finally come. So he wrote "Throwing up my head and laughing boisterously, I stalk out of my house; / How could I possibly be a commoner!" But by this time, Tang Xuanzong was no longer an emperor bent on striving for the prosperity of the country. Instead, he was given to creature comforts. Li Bai was only made a scribe hired by the imperial court to eulogize the emperor's virtues and achievements, and his political aspirations could in no way be realized. Before long, due to influential officials' jealousy and discrimination, he left Chang'an, the capital, under coercion and started to tour southern China. During this period, he wrote "Mount Skyland Ascended in a Dream—A Song of Farewell," the most representative of his works. Unable to find the way out, he strove to seek relief from illusory imagination. In his dream, he created an unusually beautiful and fascinating fairyland that was far away from secular life. In this dreamlike world, wonderful spectacles and indistinct ghastly scenes coexisted, revealing the poet's yearning for the freedom of the soul and his formidable fears of the shadows of reality. But his dream was over in a flash. Waking up, he found all the miraculous and beautiful scenes had disappeared into thin air completely. He could not help but feel depressed and perplexed. Deeply impressed by the thought that human joys were nothing but a dream that would vanish in the twinkling of an eye, Li Bai exclaimed at the end of this poem with the following proud remarks:

*How can I stoop and bow before the men in power, / And so deny myself a happy hour!*

On the other hand, Li Bai had his own way of relieving his profound sadness and frustrations that were caused by his self-confidence in his extraordinary talents and having no opportunity to put them into use. The moon and wine, the two core images and indispensable elements in his poems, played a significant role. For instance, Poem Two of "Five Poems Composed upon Visiting the Dongting Lake with My Distant Uncle Li Ye, Deputy Minister of Punishments, and Jia Zhi, an Imperial Secretary" reads:

*Not a single wisp of smoke is visible over the Dongting Lake on this autumn night; / Great it would be to go with the currents and ascend to the sky so bright. / But I may as well buy some moonlight over the Dongting Lake on credit / And row our boat to the white clouds to buy some wine.*

With rare grace and ease and natural ingenuity, this poem gives expression to the mutual communion of the poet's carefree state of mind and nature. Nature has assumed human feelings in the last two lines—"buy some moonlight over the Dongting Lake on credit" and "row our boat to the white clouds to buy some wine." With a pure and innocent heart, the poet becomes one with the earth, the sky and natural world and thus, amid the beautiful landscape, myriad thoughts and emotions well up in the poet's mind. Having extricated himself from worldly noises and disturbances, he is able to give free rein to his feelings and thoughts.

*The Drunk Taibai*, by Su Liupeng of the Qing Dynasty, represents the scene of the drunk Li Bai supported and attended by two servants in the palace of Emperor Xuanzong of Tang.

In Chinese culture the moon is imbued with a sense of mystical and obscure beauty. It can often arouse nostalgic feelings. The profound homesickness conveyed in the line "the moon viewed at home is brighter" is typical of such nostalgic feelings. Writings about the moon are innumerable in Chinese literature, in ancient myths and legends. Moreover, the Mid-Autumn Festival in Chinese culture places emphasis on family reunion, which is represented by the bright full moon. Offering sacrifices to the moon and enjoying the bright full moon are the major customs practiced at the Mid-Autumn Festival. When people gather together on the Mid-Autumn Festival night, they think of their family members and friends who are far away from home, sighing with emotion, "Over the sea grows the moon bright; / We gaze on it far, far apart." Li Bai provided the significance of the moon with even further expression in his poems. In his poem "An Ancient Ballad of the Bright Moon," he wrote about the moon thus:

*Knowing nothing about the moon in my childhood, / I called it white jade plate. / Also I wondered it might be the dressing mirror used by immortals, / Speeding along swiftly behind the white clouds.*

In this poem, Li Bai compares the moon to a plate made of white jade and the immortals, dressing mirror, which arouses both a warm feeling and a sense of mystery. In the aforementioned "Thoughts on a Tranquil Night," he states frankly that he is drowned in homesickness when he looks up at the bright moon—"Looking up, I find the moon bright; / Bowing, in homesickness I'm drowned." The poet's loneliness during his wanderings in strange lands is clearly reflected in the poem. Reading this poem, readers cannot refrain from being drowned in the poet's sadness. In another poem entitled "A Letter Written upon Hearing Wang Changling's Being Relegated to a Minor Post in Longbiao and Sent from Afar," Li Bai wrote:

*Every single poplar blossom has dropped in the crying of the cuckoos; / Shocked, I learn Longbiao is still beyond the outlandish Wuxi. / Now I send my gloomy heart to the moon bright, / Hoping, with the wind, it will reach the west of Yelang County.*

A "gloomy heart" and the "moon bright" are both sent to the poet's friend in this poem. The poet's memories of his friend after they parted and his worries about his friend's future are shown between the lines.

A painting of the poem "A Letter Written upon Hearing Wang Changling's Being Relegated to a Minor Post in Longbiao and Sent from Afar," by Sun Wenduo.

In reality Li Bai was unhappy not to have achieved his ambitions. He often gave vent to his pent-up feelings by drinking wine and singing heartily and loudly. In his youth, he was upright and chivalrous, and he also strove to follow the life of an immortal and studied Taoist doctrines. As a result, Taoist culture influenced him. His poems usually contain the messages of transcending the petty and vulgar and holding fame and official position in contempt. On the one hand, Li Bai pursued successful display of his talent in handling political affairs; on the other hand, he despised the wealth and high position that a successful official career might possibly have brought him. His thought displayed both the Confucian concept of entering society, advocating that a man should be of help to the people and his country, and the Taoist idea of renouncing human society, advocating that a man should keep himself aloof from the human world. But Li Bai had a rather complex mind which was far from being governed explicitly by these two thoughts. In one of his poems dedicated to a friend, he wrote, "Until after I've done all I can in assisting the enlightened ruler, / We'll go together and recline on the white clouds." By saying so, he expected to get a post from an enlightened emperor so as to achieve his ambitions, but he took nature, which was free from all conventions and vulgarities, as his final ideal retreat. He thought it would be better to enjoy the pleasures of life here and now. Drinking wine and enjoying the bright full moon was precisely the best way to have a free and easy sort of life.

Li Bai's poem "Drinking Alone in the Moonlight" clearly reveals to us a lonely, unrestrained romantic poet who, out of profound sadness, was pouring his own wine and diverting himself by writing poetry:

*A cup of wine, under the flowering trees; / I drink alone, for no friend is near. / Raising my cup I reckon the bright moon, / For he, with my shadow, will make three men. / The moon, alas, is no drinker of wine;*

*/ Listless, my shadow creeps about at my side. / Yet with the moon as friend and the shadow as slave / I must make merry before the Spring is spent. / To the songs I sing the moon flickers her beams; / In the dance I weave my shadow tangles and breaks. / While we were sober, three shared the fun; / Now we are drunk, each goes his way. / May we long share our odd, inanimate feast, / And meet at last on the Cloudy River of the sky.*

The romantic poet and his solitary shadow, along with the flowers, the moon, wine, singing, dancing, form a clear and beautiful scene. In the lines "Raising my cup I reckon the bright moon, / For he, with my shadow, will make three men," the poet, in the company of his own shadow, raises his cup and sings heartily and loudly under the flowering trees and the moon, hoping to forget his sorrows. Unfortunately, "The moon, alas, is no drinker of wine; / Listless, my shadow creeps about at my side," the moon has no idea why the poet gets himself drunk and his own shadow cannot understand why he is so forlorn and depressed. Naturally, the poet chooses to indulge himself in enjoying life for the time being, attempting to let his sorrows and frustrations stop haunting him. This way of settling his grievances is demonstrated in more explicit terms in his poem "Invitation to Wine," which gives an in-depth expression of the poet's indignation and resentfulness at the corrupt reality.

Amazed at Li Bai's unusual talent, wild and unruly, and unyielding character, Du Fu wrote in glowing terms thus:

*Li Bai could turn sweet nectar into verses fine; / Drunk in the capital, he'd lie in shops of wine. / Even imperial summons proudly he'd decline, / Saying immortals could not leave the drink divine.*

("Eight Immortal Drinkers")

Li Bai's poetic talent and personal charm have had a significant appeal to later generations. Many outstanding poets like Su Shi, Lu You and others all came under his influence. But Li

Bai's ingenious creative talent and unrestrained and graceful personality are far better than that of the later poets.

# Su Fu—A Compassionate Sage

In the literary history of China, Du Fu has long enjoyed equal fame with Li Bai, and the names of these two poets have been listed together as "Li and Du." Although they both lived in the High Tang period, Du Fu's poems are unlike those of Li Bai. Du Fu's poems are a crystallization of his sense of anxiety and the heavy load of responsibility he felt for the country and the future of the nation. Li Bai's poetry represents the zenith of poetic creation in the High Tang Period, whereas Du Fu's poetry has on a greater scale exerted a far-reaching influence upon the development of poetry from the mid-Tang period (766–835) to the Song Dynasty (960–1279).

In the history of the Tang Dynasty regime, the High Tang witnessed a period of extreme prosperity and unprecedented strength. Meanwhile, various social conflicts and crises also lay hidden and grew. Especially after the outbreak of the "rebellion led by An Lushan and Shi Siming," the Tang regime was unavoidably on the wane, politics became fatuous and corrupt and people lived in turmoil. With his writing brush, Du Fu gave a graphic and in-depth account of the process of change from prosperity to decline of the Tang Dynasty. His poetry is rich in terms of social content and is permeated with his deep feelings for his country and the people. Many of his works of outstanding brilliance, such as the well-acclaimed "The Three Conscripting Officers," i.e. "The Conscripting Officer at Xin'an," "The Conscripting Officer at Tongguan," "The Conscripting Officer at Shihao," and "The Lament of the New Wife," "The Old Couple Part," and "The Homeless," are true reflections of the social outlook of the Tang Dynasty when it experienced the change from the prosperity of the Kaiyuan and Tianbao periods to later decline. Owing to this, Du Fu's poetry is credited with the title "Lyrical History" by later generations.

Du Fu was the grandson of Du Shenyan, a renowned poet of the early Tang period (618–713). Having a long and profound tradition of family learning, Du Fu was fond of learning and read extensively when he was still a child. Born into an age that boasted unprecedented prosperity and vitality and raised in a family that held in high esteem the traditional culture of "revering Confucian thought and clinging to the family tradition of being officeholders," naturally he was liable to have the political ambition of "Assisting our Emperor to rule, to purify, to cleanse." He started to read poetry at seven and earned wide acclaim at fifteen for the poems he wrote. He led a wandering life of "Going off for pleasure, / Riding a horse to Qi and Zhao, wearing furs, / Leading a full and free life" ("Travel in Middle Years") when he reached twenty. He also went to Luoyang to sit the imperial examinations, but failed. What merits our attention is that, during this period, young Du Fu became acquainted with Li Bai who was then over forty years old in Luoyang. Traveling together and talking about poetry and the ways of the world, the two built profound friendly ties. Full of praise for Li Bai, Du Fu wrote many heart-stirring poems to commemorate Li Bai, such as "When love is cleft in twain by death, / A man can but try to banish his sorrow;" (Poem One of "Dreaming of Li Bai, Two Poems") "The more, because these three nights / Have I dreamed of you; and you / Seemed as real and as dear to me / As if you were beside me;" (Poem Two of "Dreaming of Li Bai, Two Poems") These lines give a vivid expression of his profound

A portrait of Du Fu, by Jiang Zhaohe.

feelings. When reading these lines, one can not help shedding tears.

At the age of thirty-five, Du Fu came to Chang'an, the then capital, hoping that his talent might be recognized by the emperor and influential officials so that he could be appointed to an official post. But this chance never came. He repeatedly presented his poems to influential officials, but his efforts proved to be fruitless. In the tenth year of Tianbao, Emperor Tang Xuanzong held sacrificial offerings to his ancestors. Taking this opportunity, Du Fu submitted three pieces of rhyme prose entitled "Greater Ode to Rites." Though Du Fu's writings were highly commended by the emperor, he was still not given an official position. It was not until several years later that he was assigned to the minor post of a military counselor. He was stranded in Chang'an for as long as ten years and was utterly frustrated. He was even haunted by the lack of food and clothing. Frustrated in life and poverty-stricken, Du Fu came into further contact with the poverty-stricken masses living at the lower strata of society and thus acquired a better understanding of them. On the other hand, he also used to serve as a companion to nobles for the sake of making a living. His frequent visits to rich and powerful families provided him with the chance of witnessing the luxurious and extravagant life of the aristocracy. The striking contrast between these two parts of society aroused an intense indignation in the poet which was fully reflected in his poems.

In his poem "Ballad of the Beautiful Ladies," Du Fu gave a portrayal of the ladies from rich families in Chang'an:

*Perfect figures showing through silk / Draperies embroidered with / Golden peacocks or silver unicorns; / Their heads dressed in kingfisher / Colors, with hanging pendants of / Cut jade; on their backs little / Overgarments studded with pearls.*

These ladies were lavishly dressed because they came from exalted families: "Amongst this galaxy the sisters / Of Concubine Yang, bearing great titles." Emperor Tang Xuanzong bestowed great favors upon the family members of Concubine Yang, his favorite concubine. Concubine Yang's two sisters were conferred the titles of "Lady Guo" and "Lady Qin." Here the poet bluntly denounced the corrupted politics of the time, pointing out that "Prime Minister Yang is all powerful, / His slightest touch will burn;" and warning the common people "Best to keep clear of him and his evil temper." These lines are expressive of the poet's bitter satire and strong indignation at the fatuous and extravagant life of the nobility.

In his long poem "Song of the Road—Going from the Capital to Fengxian," which is representative of his poems, Du Fu gave insightful and profound expression to his discontent with reality:

*The mansions burst with wine and meat; / The poor die frozen on the street. / Woe stands within an inch of weal. / Distressed, can I tell what I feel?*

The unfairness resulting from the division of society into two opposing extremes deepened Du Fu's sympathy for the common people who lived in distress and suffered from forced labor. Du Fu's major poem written during this period is "Ballad of the War Chariots," which reveals that the common people at the lower strata of society did not have enough food and clothing even though they labored assiduously and, what is more, suffered greatly from feudal obligations. They had to sacrifice their time and even their lives for the emperor's ambition of tilling the land and expanding his territory:

*Chariots rumble / And horses grumble. / The conscripts march with bow and arrows at the waist. / Their fathers, mothers, wives and children come in haste. / To see them off; the bridge is shrouded in dust*

*they've raised. / They clutch at their coats, stamp the feet and bar the way; / Their grief cries loud and strikes the cloud straight, straightaway. / An onlooker by the roadside asks an enrollee. / "The conscription is frequent," only answers he. / Some went north at fifteen to guard the river shore, / And were sent west to till the land at forty-four. / The elder bound their young heads when they went away; / Just home, they're sent to the frontier though their hair's gray. / The field on borderland becomes a sea of blood; / The emperor's greed for land is still at high flood. / Have you not heard / Two hundred districts east of the Hua Mountains lie, / Where briers and brambles grow in villages far and nigh? / Although stout women can wield the plough and the hoe, / Thorns and weeds in the east as in the west o'ergrow. / The enemy are used to hard and stubborn fight; / Our men are driven just like dogs or fowls in flight. / "You are kind to ask me. / To complain I'm not free. / In winter of this year / Conscription goes on here. / The magistrates for taxes press. / How can we pay them in distress? / If we had known sons bring no joy, / We would have preferred girl to boy. / A daughter can be wed to a neighbor, alas! / A son can only be buried under the grass! / Have you not seen / On borders green / Bleached bones since olden days unburied on the plain? / The old ghosts weep and cry, while the new ghosts complain; / The air is loud with screech and scream in gloomy rain.*

The scene of final separation between family members at the time of young men leaving home and going to fight in a distant land is truly moving: "Their fathers, mothers, wives and children come in haste. / To see them off; the bridge is shrouded in dust they've raised. / They clutch at their coats, stamp the feet and bar the way; / Their grief cries loud and strikes the cloud straight, straightaway." In the collection of *Yuefu Poems of the Han Dynasty*, there is a poem that tells the traumatic experiences of an aged soldier. The first two lines read: "At fifteen I left home to fight the foe, / And could not go back till I was four-score." ("Homecoming after War") In this poem by Du Fu, the young men were sent to fight in a distant land when they first came of age and still could not escape conscription for military service when they grew old: "The elder bound their young heads when they went away; / Just home, they're sent to the frontier though their hair's gray." The emperor was bent on expanding his territory and showed no compassion or concern for the people. The consequence of this was that the villages and land lay waste and the people were driven into dire poverty. Though deeply oppressed, people were not free to complain. They could only sigh: "If we had known sons bring no joy, / We would have preferred girl to boy. / A daughter can be wed to a neighbor, alas! / A son can only be buried under the grass!"

War was one of the major reasons that life was impossible for the people. The rebellion led by An Lushan and Shi Siming that took place in the fourteenth year of Tianbao of Tang Xuanzong's reign marked the turning point of the Tang Dynasty—from prosperity to decline, and also brought the people into deep distress. Du Fu experienced personally the turmoil of war, dashing and fleeing around. During this period, he wrote many poems which were permeated with his deep concern for the national crisis and the life of the people. "The Three Conscripting Officers," i.e. "The Conscripting Officer at Xin'an," "The Conscripting Officer at Tongguan," "The Conscripting Officer at Shihao," and "The Lament of the New Wife," "The Old Couple Part," and "The Homeless," are a series of narrative poems that give an account of the rebellion led by An Lushan and Shi Siming. These six poems give a detailed and graphic portrayal of the dilapidation of the country and the painful experiences of the people brought about by the war. Moreover, these six poems, teeming with a deep feeling of grief and remorse, are also a bitter denouncement of the cruelties of military service. The actual events described in these poems are expressive of the poet's sympathy and grief for the people. In the poem "The Conscripting Officer at Xin'an," Du Fu gives an account of the scene of a local official drafting new recruits that he witnessed in person while he was on his way:

*Traveling through Xin'an / I heard a bellowing voice / Taking roll call, and a local official / Told me how all grown lads / Had already gone, and now the call / Was for boys in their teens, many / Short and many thin, wondering / How such could help to defend cities; / As I stood I saw how the fat boys / Had mothers to farewell them, but how / Lone and pitiful the thin ones were; / Evening came, and I looked at the stream / Flowing east, heard the sound / Of sobbing from among green hills / Around; and thought it were best / For those mothers not to wither / Their eyes with weeping, for even / If eyes went to skin and bone, it would / Be to no avail; now our armies were / Besieging Yecheng, and soon it should fall; / How could we have thought the rebellion / Would drive the way it did, and our army / Scatter in retreat? Now our forces / Protect granaries, train new men, dig / Fortifications that do not go down / To water, while work on tending / Cavalry mounts is not hard, and all men / Are well fed; so no need for you to weep more! / Guo Ziyi treats his men as his / Own children.*

In order to suppress the rebellion, the imperial court enrolled new recruits successively, which heightened the load of the people who had already had their fill of trials and tribulations in life. Countless grown-ups died on the battlefields. Now undergrown teenager boys and the weak, grey-haired old men had to be recruited for fighting. The war caused countless broken families and took a heavy toll of civilians. Victims of the disaster could be found everywhere. Even the hills and the stream were grieved at the miserable sight, as is expressed in the lines "Evening came, and I looked at the stream / Flowing east, heard the sound / Of sobbing from among green hills around." However, the poet thought it was best for people not to weep, for even if their eyes went to skin and bone, it would be to no avail, and the imperial court would not alter its ruthless, heartless character.

Yang Lun, a Qing Dynasty literary critic thus commented on these six poems by Du Fu: "… Touched by the turbulence of the times he lived in, Du Fu showed profound compassion for the national crisis and grieved deeply over the dire poverty of the people…" (*Understanding Du Fu's Poetry*, volume 5). This comment characterises the major theme of most of Du Fu's poems.

The poem "Spring View" has been held in high esteem throughout the ages and, moreover, has been included in Chinese language textbooks for primary school students:

*Even though a state is crushed / Its hills and streams remain; / Now inside the walls of Chang'an / Grasses rise high among un-pruned trees; / Seeing flowers come, a flood / Of sadness overwhelms me; cut off / As I am, songs of birds stir / My heart; third month and still / Beacon fires flare as they did / Last year; to get news / From home would be worth a full / Thousand pieces of gold; / Trying to knot up my hair / I find it grey, too thin / For my pin to hold together.*

The poet's deep love of his country runs through the whole poem. The words at the beginning of the poem "A state is crushed" reveal the desolation of the country. After capturing Chang'an, the capital of the country, the rebellious forces burned and looted wantonly everywhere they went, reducing the once prosperous capital to debris and making people homeless. The lines "Seeing flowers come, a flood of sadness overwhelms me; / Cut off as I am, songs of birds stir my heart," vividly convey the poet's sadness at the sight of the flowers and birds. With the flames of the war raging far and wide for so long, many people left their homes and had no news about their family members whatsoever. The forty-six-year-old poet, who was in the prime of his life, found his hair grey and too thin to hold a light hairpin. Despite this, when the news came to him that the imperial forces had recovered lost territory, he went into raptures:

*Ballad of the War Chariots* (detail), by Xu Yansun, collection of China Art Gallery.

*News of the recovery of our lost lands / Reaches down to us in Sichuan; / Crying with happiness, my tears fall on my clothes; / I turn to see my wife and children; / Excitedly, I start to roll up my papers, / Half crazy with the good news; / Though the sun has not set, I feel I must drink and sing; / Perhaps together with the spring shall we come back home again. / Down through the Yangtze Gorges shall we sweep, / Then on to Xiangyang, finally arriving in old Luoyang.*

("Good News of the Recovery of the Central Plains")

The poet's feelings always rose and fell along with the fate of his country and the people. His benevolent broad-mindedness is revealed in his poems.

Having no regular residence in his old age, Du Fu had to bring all his family and drift along from place to place. At fifty-nine, he died of an illness in a small boat on the Xiangjiang River. Throughout his life, he suffered many setbacks and experienced fully the trials of life, and at times he even did not have enough food and clothing. Having no one to turn to, he spent his last years in great misery. He even experienced the sorrow of losing his youngest son, who died of hunger in childhood. However, what is conveyed in his poems is not his own bitterness, but

The Museum of Du Fu thatched cottage in Chengdu was Du Fu's home during his exile. Du Fu enjoyed years of peace and stability at this home, and the seven-character poetry written during this period is particularly skilled.

his deep concern and care for his country and the people. When the straw from his thatched cottage was rolled up by the autumn gales, he exclaimed, "Could I get mansions covering ten thousand miles, I'd house all scholars poor and make them beam with smiles. In wind and rain these mansions would stand like mountains high!" If only this could be, he continued, "I would be content to see my poor unroofed cottage demolished, with I myself frozen to death." ("My Cottage Unroofed by Autumn Gales")

Pu Qilong, a literary critic from the Qing Dynasty, made the following commentary on Du Fu's poetry: "Du Fu's poems are expressions of his own temperament and feelings, yet they cover all the aspects of social life under the three emperors' reigns, Tang Xuanzong, Tang Suzong and Tang Daizong" (*Reading Du Fu with Heart*). Du Fu's poetry touches upon various issues concerning politics, economy, military affairs, and daily life under three emperors' reigns during the Tang Dynasty. More importantly, the poet's true feelings run through all his poems. With his Confucian, scholarly, compassionate broad-mindedness, Du Fu carried forward and developed the realistic literary tradition starting from *The Book of Songs* onwards, and formed an important connecting link in terms of the development of ancient

Chinese poetry between the preceding and the succeeding poets. From the Song Dynasty onwards, Du Fu's poetry has drawn extensive attention and has been studied nationwide. Honored with the title "Sage Poet" by the later generations, Du Fu has been regarded as a model of sages who exercised a significant influence on the history of Chinese literature.

The Tang Dynasty was the golden age of feudal China, as well as a glorious peak in the history of Chinese literature. Poetry was the most typical literary form of the Tang Dynasty. However, Tang poetry experienced a fall from its zenith to decline from the mid-Tang onwards. By the late Tang period, a trend of decadence and beauty began to take shape in poetry.

In the Tang Dynasty, there were not only great poets like Li Bai and Du Fu who shine through the ages, but also a large number of outstanding poets like Wang Wei (701–761), Meng Haoran (689–740), Bai Juyi (772–846), Li He (790–816), Li Shangyin (813–858), and Du Mu (803–853). Bai Juyi, a poet of great renown, was good at writing allegorical poems. He argued that poems and essays must serve the fast-changing times and real life. His poems satirize excessive taxes and levies, protest against militarism and attack the rich and dignitaries. The language of his poems is fluid, easy to understand, vivid and moving. Li Shangyin (813–858) and Du Mu (803–853) represented the highest attainment in poetry in the late Tang period. Comparing them to Li Bai and Du Fu, later generations referred to them jointly as "Li and Du the Junior." Li Shangyin's poems are characterized by an evocative, beautiful style. His untitled love poems, especially those that voice his personal sentiments, have long been highly acclaimed. Some of the beautiful and concise lines from his poetry were even set to music and have been widely circulated and sung. For instance, the lines "Spring silkworm till its death spins silk from lovesick heart; / Candles only when burned have no tears to shed," and "Having no wings, I can't fly to you as I please; / Our hearts as one, your ears can hear my inner call," have become established expressions frequently used by men and women in love to profess their feelings. What is more, the line "Our hearts as one, your ears can hear my inner call" has become a set phrase in the Chinese language expressing that two hearts have a common beat and are linked together. Du Mu's poems are graceful and tasteful, refreshing and vigorous with a tinge of natural charm in style. "The Mourning Day" is the most widely known of his poems:

*A drizzling rain falls like tears on the Mourning Day; / The mourner's heart is going to break on his way. / Where can a wine shop be found to drown his sad hours? / A cowherd points to a cot 'mid apricot flowers.*

The poem gives a brilliant sketch of the mourner journeying on his way in the drizzling rain.

Great in number, diverse in style, superb in quality and covering a wide range of subjects, Tang poetry has had a far-reaching influence on the creative writing of later generations.

# *Ci* Poetry

## Poems That Can Be Sung

*Ci* poetry, originating from among the people, was a new form of literary writing in the Tang Dynasty and was fully developed in the Song Dynasty (960–1279). The Five Dynasties and Ten States period (907–960) was an important phase for the establishment and development of *ci* poetry. *Ci*, originally referring to the words of a song and called "words to a tune" during the Five Dynasties, are lyrics that are supposed to be set to music. Each *ci* has a fixed tune of its own. Mostly divided into the upper part and the lower part, the lines of *ci* are different in length. Therefore, *ci* is also called "Short and long lines." Compared with traditional poetry, *ci* has a narrower theme which is usually limited to writing about love affairs and women's sorrows. It is often flowery in language and sorrowful in artistic style. This writing style did not take on a new look until Su Shi and some others from the Song Dynasty had had it tastefully furnished.

Wen Tingyun, the founder of the Flower School, had a great influence on the later "subtle and implicit school" of *ci* poetry.

The Five-Dynasty period of the Late Tang Dynasty saw social disorder and decline of the state, bringing increasingly serious damage both to economy and culture. Despite this, several comparatively stable separatist regimes came into being in southern China where sat the Five Dynasties and Ten States. The relatively independent and stable political situation and the people's indulgence in feasting and pleasure-seeking in their separate states provided the breeding ground for the development of this writing style suitable for expressing sensual pleasure and merry-making. Under such circumstances, two *ci* centers took shape, one in Western Shu, the other in Southern Tang.

The Western Shu School of *ci* poetry was usually called the Flower School. It referred to the group of *ci* poets included in *Among the Flowers*, an anthology of *ci* poems selected and compiled by Zhao Chongza of the Later Shu period. Wen Tingyun (whose dates of birth and death remain unknown, c. 812–870) and Wei Zhuang (836–910) were representative *ci* poets of the Flower School. Wen Tingyun, whose style name was Feiqing, achieved outstanding accomplishments in the fields of writing poetry, *ci* poetry and descriptive poetic prose. His poems are equally famous with those by Li Shangyin, and he and Li Shangyin were jointly referred to as "Wen and Li." Viewed from the perspective of *ci* poetry, Wen Tingyun was respected as the founder of the Flower School. He was the first poet who concentrated on writing words for tunes. He basically established the traditional writing style of *ci* poetry in terms of language, form and theme, which is flowery, sensual and sumptuous. "Pusaman" is the best known of all his *ci* poems:

*Like ranges of mountain, / The screen flickers in morning sunlight. / Cloud-like black hair over her temples / Flows down sweet-smelling fair cheeks in disarray. / Listlessly getting out of bed, she paints eyebrows. / Sluggishly, she washes and dresses. / In the mirror are her beautiful face and flowers, / Her beauty putting the flowers to shame. / Thin silk dress shines with fine embroideries, / Two golden francolins, a loving couple.*

Wei Zhuang has enjoyed equal reputation with Wen Tingyun. Wei Zhuang's *ci* poems are gentle, graceful, charming and light in style, with a tinge of refreshing brightness. Compared with Wen Tingyun, Wei Zhuang's *ci* poems are richer in content. It can be stated that Wei Zhuang's style differs from the other *ci* poets of the Flower School. The following *ci* poem "Pusaman" by Wei Zhuang can best represent his writing style:

*Everybody says Jiangnan is an alluring land. / Travellers should only stay till they're in age advanced. / The creeks in spring are bluer than the sky, / In a pleasure boat one falls asleep, / Listening to the rain-patter light.*

*Night Banquet of Han Xizai* (detail), by Gu Hongzhong of the Five Dynasties. This painting vividly depicts the extravagant lives of upper class scholars of the Southern Tang. Collection of the Palace Museum, Beijing.

*By the fire the woman like moonlight glows, / Her lily-white arms are like piles of snow. / So do not go home ere one is old, / For if you do, your heart would turn cold.*

The flourishing of the Southern Tang *ci* poetry came slightly later than that of the Western Shu period. Like Western Shu, the Southern Tang Dynasty also acquired a relatively independent political situation that was cut off from the outside world in the time of turbulence and formed a culture of its own with strong local characteristics. The major *ci* poets of the Southern Tang Dynasty include Li Jing the father (916–961) (also known as Zhongzhu), Li Yu the son (937–978) (also known as Houzhu) and Feng Yansi (903–960), the prime minister. Li Yu was the last emperor of the Southern Tang Dynasty, and was later popularly called "Li the Last Emperor." By the time he succeeded to the throne, the Southern Tang Dynasty had acknowledged the legal status of the Song Dynasty and had to seek temporary security in reduced territory. In the eighth year of the Kaibao (974) of the Song Dynasty, the Song troops seized the capital of Southern Tang. "Li the Last Emperor" was stripped off his garments and surrendered to the Song army. As a captive, he was taken to

Bianjing and was granted the title of "Marquis of Disobeying Orders." In terms of style, Li Yu's earlier *ci* poems, which depict the luxury and extravagance of life within the imperial palace, are resplendently lofty with the traces of beauty typical of the Flower School, and at the same time gentle and charming with a trace of tolerance. These *ci* poems vividly reflect the breadth of mind, temperaments and tastes, as well as the deep emotions and unconventional spirits of this bold, easy and elegant young emperor. On the contrary, by making a clean sweep of gentleness and charm, he gives a plain account of feelings in his *ci* poems of the later stage. Moreover, his heart-felt feelings and profound grievances expressed in these *ci* poems give rise to the solemn and magnificent appearance of a monarch eaten up by sorrow and resentment. "Xiangjianhuan" reads thus:

*All the flowers faded, / So hasty! / Alas! Heartless cold drizzling in morning, / And strong wind at night.*

*Tears of rouge, withered blossoms, / Why insisting on my staying for wine? / Who knows when will you bloom next time? / Eternal sorrow always goes together with life, / Like the water flowing east forever.*

## Su Shi

When it came to the time of Su Shi, the style of *ci* poetry took on a new outlook. Su Shi formed a free and powerful *ci* style, which was further developed by Xin Qiji of the Southern Song Dynasty. Su Shi (1037–1101), style name Zizhan and alias Dongpo, was a native of Meishan, Sichuan. He claimed outstanding distinctions in the literary creation of poetry, *ci* poetry and prose. He had a long and profound tradition of family learning. His father, Su Xun, had been a scholar of great renown and his mother guided him into reading the *History of Han*. Exceedingly bright from his childhood, he had great knowledge and was a man of many talents. At twenty, he became a successful candidate in the highest civil service imperial examination. He successively held the position of Member of the Imperial Academy and was concurrently Minister of War and an official in charge of collations and such like. But, as he opposed the reform instituted by Wang Anshi, he was banished from the court and exiled to remote regions several times, the farthest one being Qiongzhou, present-day Hainan Island. Su Shi's works consist of *The Complete Works of Dongpo* which consists of more than a hundred volumes, over two thousand and seven hundred poems, over three hundred *ci* poems and a considerable amount of prose works.

A portrait of Su Shi.

*Ci* poetry stemmed from among the people and became popular with courtesans. It had long been looked upon as a tool for leisure and amusement, playing the role of adding joys and pressing people to more wine. Su Shi broadened the scope of *ci* poetry. Maintaining that "poetry is a type of *ci*," he added the spirit of poetry to the outer form of *ci*. Su Shi is usually believed to be the founder of the free and powerful *ci* school. The words "free and powerful" refer in particular to two aspects, one is the style and the other the *ci* poets' temperaments and tastes conveyed in their *ci* poems. Liu Xizai said in his *A Survey of Art: On Ci Poetry*, "If viewed from the perspective of effectively putting into practice the idea that no meaning cannot be expressed in poetry, and no event cannot be translated into poetry, Dongpo is analogous to Du Fu. If viewed from the perspective of the free and powerful style of writing, Dongpo is similar to Li Bai." Breaking through the limitation that *ci* poetry could only express women's feelings of sadness and bitter sorrow for want of love, Su Shi put into practice his idea that everything can be expressed in poetry. As a result, a wide range of the subject matter conventional poets cover in their poetry, such as thoughts on the past, criticizing current politics and government, mourning for the deceased, and praising pastoral life, all find adequate expression in Su Shi's *ci* poems. Therefore, his *ci* poems are exceedingly rich and varied. Surging waves, marble towers and jade halls, farm houses and country estates, and galloping chariots are all written in the *ci* form. Lu You thus commented on Su Shi in the fifth volume of his *Notes of an Aged Scholar*:

*Common views have it that Dongpo was incapable of writing rhymed verses. So most of the verse he composed in the Yuefu form followed no regular meter and rhyme schemes. Chao Yidao wrote, "At the beginning of Shaosheng period, Dongpo and I parted in Bianjing. At the farewell party, he got drunk and chanted a song to the tune of 'Guyangguan.'" From this we learn it's improper to say Dongpo could not chant to regular meter and rhyme schemes. He was just free and unrestrained in character and was unwilling to accommodate himself with rhyme schemes. I had a try at reading his ci poetry, and was deeply touched by its power and grandeur.*

This comment gives an explanation to Su Shi's "free and powerful style" from the perspective of his temperaments. Seen from Lu You's account of Su Shi, it's not that Su Shi did not know the rules of meter and rhyme schemes, but that he was just free and unrestrained in character and was unwilling to be confined to the meters and rhyme schemes. This is why his *ci* poetry always followed his mind and kept free from regular rhyme schemes. There are only a small proportion of *ci* poems typical of the "free and powerful" style among Su Shi's three hundred odd *ci* poems, yet they presaged the new way of development of *ci*

*Scroll on Red Cliff*, by Wu Yuanzhi of the Nurchen Jin Dynasty, collection of the Palace Museum, Taipei. It represents the scene of Su Shi boating with friends in Chibi (Red Cliff).

poetry. Viewed from the perspective of language style, Su Shi got rid of the ornate expressions much used by the *ci* poets prior to him, and absorbed lines from the poems of Tao Yuanming, Li Bai, Du Fu, Han Yu and so on in writing *ci* poems of his own. Apart from this, he used very few colloquialisms, making his *ci* poems refreshing and graceful.

"Niannujiao: Memories of the Past at Red Cliff" is the most famous piece among his *ci* poems with a free and powerful style. This *ci* poem was written in Hangzhou when Su Shi reached middle age and had been repeatedly banished from office. It is alleged that while Su Shi was serving as Member of the Imperial Academy, he asked his aide, "What is your opinion of my *ci* poems and Liu Yong's?" Su Shi's aide answered, "Liu Yong's *ci* poems are fit for girls of eighteen or seventeen who, holding red ivory clappers, sing 'The riverside is strewn with willow trees, the morning breeze wafts in with a waning moon.' Your Excellency's *ci* poems are fit for big fellows from northwestern China who, playing a bronze *pipa* or iron clappers, chant 'East flows the mighty river.'" "East flows the mighty river" is a famous quotation from "Niannujiao: Memories of the Past at Red Cliff:"

*East flows the mighty river, / Sweeping away the heroes of time past; / This ancient rampart on its western shore / Is Zhou Yu's Red Cliff of Three Kingdoms' fame; / Here jagged boulders pound the clouds, / Huge waves tear banks apart, / And foam piles up a thousand drifts of snow; / A scene fair as a painting, / Countless the brave men here in time gone by!*

*I dream of Marshal Zhou Yu in his day / With his new bride, the Lord Qiao's younger daughter, / Dashing and debonair, / Silk-capped, with feather fan, / He laughed and jested / While the dread enemy fleet was burned to ashes! / In fancy through those scenes of old I range. / My heart overflowing, surely a figure of fun. / A man gray before his time. / Ah, this life is a dream, / Let me drink to the moon on the river!*

A painting of the *ci* poem "Shuidiaogetou," by Liu Dawei.

Because Su Shi was against the reform instituted by Wang Anshi, he was banished from the imperial court to Huangzhou (present-day Huanggang, Hubei Province). He visited Red Cliff (Chibi) twice, which lies on the outskirts of Huangzhou, and wrote two descriptive poetic prose works as well as this *ci* poem. The line mentioned in this *ci* poem "Zhou Yu's Red Cliff of Three Kingdoms' fame" refers to the historical event during the Three Kingdoms period—Zhou Yu, Marshal of the Kingdom of Eastern Wu, routed Cao Cao's troops at Red Cliff. The exact place where Zhou Yu triumphed over Cao Cao was near Jiayu of Hubei Province, not the Red Cliff near Huangzhou. With a sudden rush of inspiration Su Shi wrote this *ci* poem to give vent to his feelings. The description of the scene by the river "Here jagged boulders pound the clouds, / Huge waves tear banks apart, / And foam piles up a thousand drifts of snow," really gives the readers a feeling that the scene is as fair as a painting, and is a magnificent sight too. Red Cliff, the land of ancient Eastern Wu, was the place where Zhou Yu had rendered meritorious service and made a distinguished career. Su Shi was deeply filled with admiration for Zhou Yu's dashing and debonair character. In this *ci* poem Su Shi sighs that he has accomplished nothing in life but his hair has turned gray, imaging if Zhou Yu's soul revisits this land and meets him, surely he will be a figure of fun in the eyes of Zhou Yu. So Su Shi laments "Ah, this life is a dream." Literary critics of the later generations held the opinion that the title of this *ci* poem is to express memories of the past, but the *ci* poem itself expresses that the poet's ambitions have been completely whiled away in real life. In this *ci* poem, Su Shi reminisces about the heroic deeds of the old generation and sighs over his having accomplished nothing. However, he is also able to find the way out of Zhuangzi's and Buddhist thoughts, and come to the conclusion that this life is a dream. Therefore, this *ci* poem can in no way disguise the poet's optimistic attitude and initiative.

Su Shi's aspiration to render meritorious service to the country is more clearly expressed in another famous *ci* poem entitled "Jiangchengzi: Hunting at Mizhou:"

*Old limbs regain the fire of youth: / Left hand leashing a hound, / On the right wrist a falcon. / Silk-capped and sable-coated, / A thousand horsemen sweep across the plain; / The whole city, it is said, has turned out / To watch His Excellency / Shoot the tiger!*

*Heart gladdened by wine, / Who cares / For a few white hairs? / But when will the court send an envoy / With an imperial tally to pardon the exile? / That day I will bend my bow like a full moon / And aiming northwest / Shoot down the Wolf from the sky!*

The line "Heart gladdened by wine" gives a full and accurate expression of the poet's "free and powerful"style. What is more, the style of this *ci* poem as a whole varies drastically with the over-cautiousness of the *ci* poems written since the late Tang Dynasty and the Five Dynasties.

"Shuidiaogetou: Bright Moon, When Was Your Birth?" is another well-known *ci* poem by Su Shi written in a free and powerful style:

*Bright moon, when was your birth? / Wine cup in hand, I ask the deep blue sky; / Not knowing what year it is tonight / In those celestial palaces on high. / I long to fly back on the wind, / Yet dread those crystal towers, those courts of jade, / Freezing to death among those icy heights! / Instead I rise to dance with my pale shadow; / Better off, after all, in the world of men.*

*Rounding the red pavilion, / Stooping to look through gauze windows, / She shines on the sleepless. / The moon should know no sadness; / Why, then, is she always full when dear ones are parted? / For men the grief of parting, joy of reunion, / Just as the moon wanes and waxes, is bright or dim; / Always some flaw—and so it has been since of old, / My one wish for you, then, is long life / And a share in this loveliness far, far away!*

# Li Qingzhao

Li Qingzhao (1084–c. 1155), alias Yi'an, was a native of Shandong. She is one of the very few known female writers in the history of Chinese literature. Her father, Li Gefei, won recognition from Su Shi for the literary merit of his prose, and her mother Wang was also well educated. Li Qingzhao earned a name for her poems from childhood. At the age of nineteen, she married Zhao Mingcheng, an Imperial College graduate. Having similar temperaments and tastes, they were both fond of collecting inscriptions on ancient bronzes and stone tablets and collating ancient classics. Taking

A portrait of Li Qingzhao.

delight in reading, and writing and responding to poems by each other, they had a very happy life. In the first year of Jianyan (1127), she and Zhao Mingcheng fled south. Most of their inscriptions on ancient bronzes and stone tablets, calligraphies and paintings they had collected during the past years were lost in the turmoil of the war. After Zhao Mingcheng died of illness, Li Qingzhao led a wandering life in the regions of Hangzhou, Yuezhou and Jinhua and spent her remaining years in loneliness and misery. Marked by the change of her life and her fleeing south, Li Qingzhao's *ci* poems were divided into two periods.

The life of a girl and a young woman is the main theme of her *ci* poems from the first period. *"Rumengling"* recounts her girlhood experience of getting drunk on an outing:

*I often remember that sunset at Creek Pavilion: / Too drunk to know our way back home. / Turning the boat round after a joyous day, / We blundered deeper into lotus' way. / Punt away! / Punt away! / We drove up a beachful of herons and gulls.*

She stayed out till it was very late. Moreover, she got too drunk to find her way home. As a result, she blundered deeper into the lotus' way. As she was eager to look for her way home, she drove up a beachful of herons and gulls who were about to go to sleep. A girl, lost out of drunkenness, could display such high spirits when she recalled this experience of hers. This shows that she was bold and innocent, carefree and lively by nature. Most daughters from families of good social standing in her time were confined to their homes and were not permitted to go outdoors. This suggests the relaxed environment in Li Qingzhao's own family.

After she was married, as she was not allowed to go with her husband when he left home and went to his post, she expressed her love for her husband in her *ci* poems in a forthright way. For this, she was criticized by others who commented, "Never before did a woman from an official family write so immorally." The following is one of her *ci* poems expressing her love for her husband:

*Veiled in thin mist and thick cloud, how sad the long day! / Incense from golden censer melts away. / The double Ninth comes again; / Alone I still remain / In silken bed curtain, on pillow smooth like jade. / Feeling the midnight chill invade.*

*At dusk I drink before chrysanthemums in bloom, / My sleeves filled with fragrance and gloom. / Say not my soul / Is not consumed. Should the west wind uproll / The curtain of my bower, / You'll see a face thinner than yellow flower.*

Starting from the first year of Jingkang (1126) onwards, Li Qingzhao suffered from the pains of the fall of her country, the breakup of her family and the death of her husband, and led a wandering life for a long period of time. Her *ci* poems written in this period mainly recount her wretched existence. But some of the lines from these *ci* poems also give expression to the common

A painting on the *ci* poem "Rumengling."

feelings of the refugees who fled south, such as "Where my native place is I'll never forget, / Unless I'm drunk," and "Heart-broken on my pillow, I hear midnight rain / Drizzling now and again. / It saddens a Northern woman who sighs. / What can she do, unused to it, but rise?" Generally speaking, Li Qingzhao knew consciously which literary form would fit in perfectly with her writing. She mainly expressed her pent-up feeling of sadness in her *ci* poems and left her deeper and more expansive thoughts aside to be dealt with in her poems. "Shengshengman: Seeking, Seeking," a masterpiece of *ci* poems written after she fled south, is famous for her description of sorrow:

*Seeking, seeking, / Chilly and quiet, / Desolate, painful and miserable. / Even when it's warmer there is still a chill, / It is most difficult to keep well. / Three or two cups of light wine, / How can they ward off the strong morning wind? / Wild geese fly past, while I'm broken-hearted; / But I recognize they are my old friends.*

*Fallen chrysanthemums piled up on the ground, / So withered, / Who would pluck them? / Leaning on the window, / How can I pass the time till night alone? / The drizzle falls on the wutong trees, / Rain-drops drip down at dusk. / At a time like this, / What immense sorrow I must bear!*

This *ci* poem displays the poetess' anguish over the fall of her country, the sorrow of a widow and the hardships of drifting from one place to another for a living and is imbued with a strong sense of profundity and heavy-heartedness. In the lingering cold it is hard to keep fit. The light wine, the assault of the evening gusts in autumn and piles of withered and fallen chrysanthemums jointly present a world of immense sorrow. Li Qingzhao's *ci* poems give voice to her profound sadness and grief. "Desolate, painful and miserable" feelings remain the constant theme of her *ci* poems. However, through her poems, she conveys her heroic spirit and lofty sentiments as revealed in her poem "A Quatrain:"

*Be man of men while you're alive; / Be soul of souls if you were dead! / Thinking of Xiang Yu who'd not survive / His men whose blood for him was shed!*

and her indignation as revealed in the lines "Not a single man like Wang Dao is attainable in this strange land in the south; / Neither a Liu Kun on my lost land the north."

Li Qingzhao's *ci* poems mainly covered the theme of love and life, expressing inner emotional feelings from the perspective of a women's sensitivity. Marked by veiled and gentle, graceful and lively feminine beauty, her *ci* poems won her the name "founder of *ci* poetry in a subtle and implicit style." The term "subtle and implicit" as a style of *ci* poetry came into being in a later time. During the Song Dynasty in which Li Qingzhao lived, people used the terms such as the "Flower School," the "Southern Tang Style," "Liu Yong Style," and "Yi'an Style" to refer to the different styles of *ci* poetry. Up to the Ming Dynasty, some people put forth the saying, "Roughly speaking, *ci* poems are marked by two different styles, one is the subtle and implicit, the other the free and powerful." Henceforth, people gradually started to comment on *ci* poems by using the terms "free and powerful" and "subtle and implicit." The source of the term "subtle and implicit" is from the lines *in Remarks of Monarchs: The State of Wu (Guoyu: Wuyu)*, which read as follows: "Since you know well the monarch is a headstrong man of authority, you should be 'subtle and implicit' in speech so as to comply with him." The original meaning of the term, "subtle and implicit" refers to women's humbleness, compliance, and agreeability in speech. If we view the conclusive judgment "Li Qingzhao is the founder of *ci* poetry in a subtle and implicit style," in the light of this definition of the term "subtle and implicit," it is likely that we need to pay a little more attention to the poetess' treatment of genres. In other words, Li Qingzhao's *ci* poems, particularly those written in the later period, are indeed subtle, restrained and mournful, but she was just adopting the *ci* form for the purpose of giving vent to her profound sorrow. To get an overall view and a better understanding of the poetess and her writings, it is necessary for us to link her *ci* poems with her other poems and prose writings.

# Xin Qiji

Xin Qiji (1140–1207), style name You'an and alias Jiaxuan, authored *Short and Long Lines of Jiaxuan*, which consists of twelve volumes. He was born in Ji'nan and grew up in a time when Central China was falling into the enemy hands. The sufferings the northern people had experienced left a deep impression on him. In 1161, when Wanyan Liang, the emperor of Jin, forged ahead south to invade the Southern Song, Xin Qiji organized a contingent of two thousand people and joined the forces of resistance against

A portrait of Xin Qiji.

Jin led by the peasants' leader, Geng Jing. Later Geng Jing was killed by a traitor named Zhang Anguo. Xin Qiji led fifty cavalries into the Jin military barracks of fifty thousand soldiers, and captured alive the traitor Zhang Anguo, called an army of around ten thousand people to cross over to his side and led them to the Southern Song. In spite of this, he was never really entrusted with any important position by the Southern Song court.

Though a lower-ranking official of the Southern Song Dynasty, he concerned himself with the safety of his motherland. He wrote and submitted his memorials to the Southern Song emperor, Song Xiaozong, and advocated fighting against the invading enemy from the north. But his proposals never received a response. Nonetheless, he held fast to his stand of loving his country and protecting the people. While serving as an official in Hunan, Hubei, Jiangxi, and Fujian, he adopted numerous measures of building up the strength of the nation and enriching its people. While he served as the governor of Zhenjiang in his remaining years, he was still energetically making preparations for war. By this time it had been forty-three years since he went south. At the time when the Southern Song was defeated, he suffered from misunderstanding and vilification and died from sorrow. The following is a comment on Xin Qiji by later generations: "Though he was as talented as Guan Zhong and Yue Yi, he was denied the opportunities to bring his talent into full play. The pent-up faithfulness and indignation burning in him found no outlet. Take a look at his 'Pozhenzi: A Poem in a Heroic Vein for Chen Tongfu,' a *ci* poem in response to Chen Tongfu's. What a man he was! Hence, he aired all of his heroic spirit and lofty sentiments as well as his depression through his *ci* poems." *Ci* is the basic form Xin Qiji employed to express his feelings. More than six hundred and twenty *ci* poems by Xin Qiji survive today.

As Xin Qiji had personally fought in the battles against Jin troops, he appeared to be totally different from those frail-looking intellectuals of his time. In his *ci* poems, he showed admiration for awe-inspiring and vigorous men alone, eulogizing Liu Yu's northern expedition as "As a tiger to swallow up vast territories;" and depicting his youthful ambitions as "With every ounce of my strength, I brandish my spear," "Arching across the sky, swallow up Cao Cao and capture Liu Bei." Lines depicting battle scenes also appeared in his *ci* poems constantly, such as "Horses sped as if on wings, / Bow-strings twanged like

A painting on the *ci* poem "Yongyule: Thinking of the Past at Beigu Pavilion in Jingkou," by Wang Guoxin.

thunder," "The foe prepared their silver shafts during the nights; / During the days we shot arrows from golden quiver." The *ci* poems he wrote in his later years were filled with more thoughts of King Yu's great deeds, as expressed in the lines "Great deeds live on ten thousand generations; / Hard he toiled in ancient times."

When he served as governor of Zhenjiang, Xin Qiji was over fifty years old. But his soaring ambition of recovering the lost territory in the north never faded. During this period, he wrote "Yongyule: Thinking of the Past at Beigu Pavilion in Jingkou" to express his noble aspirations:

*In this ancient land / What trace remains of Wu's brave king Sun Quan? / Towers and pavilions where girls danced and sang, / Your glory is swept away by wind and rain; / The slanting sunlight falls on grass and trees, / Small lanes, the quarters of the humble folk; / Yet here, they say, Liu Yu lived. / I think of the days gone by / When with gilded spear and iron-clad steed he charged / Like a tiger to swallow up vast territories.*

*In the days of Yuanjia / Hasty preparations were made / To march to the Langjuxu Mountains, / Now forty-three years have passed, / And looking north I remember / The beacon fires that blazed the way to Yangzhou; / Bitter memories these / Of sacred crows among the holy drums / In the Tartar emperor's temple. / Who will ask old Lian Po / If he still enjoys his food?*

Deeply discontented with the Southern Song's policy of seeking temporary security in reduced territory, he ridiculed the regime in the line "Dwindling stream and meager hills were not much to look at," and expressed his worries in the lines "On overhanging rails where the setting sun sees / Heartbroken willow trees!" The men in power in the Southern Song court were those who felt proud of fickle fame and were like the dust floating about in a ray of sunlight as is expressed in the lines "Gazing on the dust in the ray of sunlight coming in through a crack of the door, / It suddenly dawned on me chaos prevails everywhere in our human world." "Shuilongyin: On Riverside Tower at Jiankang," also one of Xin Qiji's well-known *ci* poems, expressed his anguish and grief over the tottering Southern Song regime:

*The southern sky for miles and miles in autumn dye / And boundless autumn water spread to meet the sky. / I gaze on far-off northern hills / Like spiral shells or hair décor of jade, / Which grief or hatred overfills. / Leaning at sunset on balustrade / And hearing a lonely swan's song, / A wanderer on southern land, / I look at my precious sword long, / And pound all the railings with my hand, / But nobody knows why / I climb the tower high.*

*Don't say for food / The perch is good! / When west winds blow, / Why don't I homeward go? / I'd be ashamed to see the patriot, / Should I retire to seek for land and cot. / I sigh for passing years I can't retain; / In driving wind and blinding rain / Even an old tree grieves. / To whom then may I say / To wipe my tears away / With her pink handkerchief or her green sleeves?*

Xin Qiji carried forward the free and powerful *ci* style started by Su Shi. Depictions of grand scenes and heroic battles remained the major subject matter of his *ci* poems. Even objects were depicted with firm and unyielding wills, such as "the ten thousand *li* long sword across the sky," "one thousand *zhang* rainbow bridge," and the potted narcissus landscape "bathing in ten thousand acres of misty water." In his writings, Xin Qiji expressed his feelings, described scenery and objects, recorded events and developed arguments. By taking advantage of the merits of various literary forms like poetry, prose and descriptive poetic prose, he enriched the use of language in the art of *ci* poetry, thus establishing its free and powerful style and making it stand out among other forms of literary creation.

Xin Qiji was adept at integrating literary allusions into his *ci* poems, quoting extensively from Confucian classics, historical books, works of the various schools of thought during the period from Pre-Qin to the early Han Dynasty, elegies of Chu as well as Li Bai and Du Fu's poems, and Han Yu and Liu Zongyuan's prose writings. Those who favored him thought that Xin Qiji used these allusions for the purpose of using the past to disparage the present and that "An allusion used appropriately is like the writer's own creation," - a conception developed by Liu Xie in his *Dragon-Carving and the Literary Mind: Allusions*. Those who were against him held the opinion that he was just showing off his erudition. In the use of language, Xin Qiji not only used the sentence patterns typical of the "ancient style" and "modern style" poetry as Su Shi had done, he also absorbed into his *ci* poems the styles of prose, rhythmical prose characterized by parallelism and ornateness, and folk idioms, thus providing his *ci* poems with broader scope for expression.

# Two Outstanding Playwrights of Yuan Opera

## Guan Hanqing and Wang Shifu

# Guan Hanqing

The birth of the Yuan Opera (otherwise known as Yuan *za ju*) marked the entry of Chinese opera into a golden age. As the most important playwright of the Yuan Opera, Guan Hanqing (whose dates of birth and death unknown) was very active during the thirteenth century in north China, spending most of his time in the grand capital of the Yuan Dynasty (present-day Beijing). Of the sixty plays he wrote, a dozen or more have survived, among them, *Snow in Midsummer (Dou'e Yuan)*, *The Riverside Pavilion (Wang Jiang Ting)* and *Lord Guan Goes to the Feast (Dan Dao Hui)*, still being staged today. The World Peace Council nominated Guan Hanqing a world famous artist in 1958, and the Concise Britannica Encyclopedia describes him as "the greatest playwright in China, widely acknowledged in literary and art circles." So far, his works have been translated into English, French, German, and Japanese.

Unlike other Confucian scholars, Guan Hanqing was unconventional, very relaxed and elegant in bearing, considered to have a "dubious character" by some. He had a lot of life experience, having practiced medicine, once serving as an imperial physician for the Jin-Dynasty court. The Mongolian Yuan Dynasty considered the Han Chinese to be very low in social status. As it was impossible to pursue a political career, most Han scholars found themselves in story-telling troupes, mixing with people even lower in social status, writing plays or story scripts as an outlet for their talent. Having no access to officialdom, Guan Hanqing

A portrait of Guan Hanqing, by Li Hu, collection of the National Museum of China.

was the most well known in a story group called Yujing. He was very knowledgeable and versatile, quick witted, humorous, excellent at composing, good at singing, dancing and musical temperament, working as a playwright, an actor, and a manager of a troupe at the same time. In these years, actresses in troupes were often also prostitutes. Guan Hanqing got along with them quite well. Zhu Lianxiu, an actress and a prostitute in one, was his intimate friend. As the head a performing troupe, Guan Hanqing styled himself as "a bronze pea," a nickname people gave to experienced brothel frequenters. However, this "bronze pea," he said, was able to withstand all kinds of suffering - steaming, boiling, grinding, and frying.

Many of Guan Hanqing's works were comedies. *The Riverside Pavilion* is one, full of acid satire on a young lord surnamed Yang, nothing but a womanizer and a drinker. Even in *Snow in Midsummer*, the tragedy he wrote in later years, comic gestures are found.

As Guan Hanqing's representative work, *Snow in Midsummer* tells a heart-wrending story about a woman named Dou'e. Her father is a poor scholar. Before he sets off for the capital to attend the royal examinations to attain an official position, he asks Old Woman Cai, a money-lender, to take care of his daughter. Actually, this makes Dou'e her daughter-in-law as payment of a loan. Before long, Dou'e's husband dies, leaving only the old woman and Dou'e behind. When the old woman is almost killed, Zhang Lüer and his father save her. On learning that the old woman and her daughter-in-law are both widowed, the father and son, both being widowers, press the old woman for marriages:

*Zhang Lüer: Did you hear that dad? She has a daughter-in-law at home. Suppose you take her as your wife and I take the daughter-in-law? Propose it to her, dad.*

*Zhang Lüer's father: Hey, widow! You've no husband and I've no wife. How about the two of us getting married?*

Brick engravings of *za ju* scenes from the Jin Tombs of Jishan, Shanxi. They vividly portray the gestures and expressions of dramatic figures, and thus reflect the history of the flourishing *za ju*.

*The old woman: What an idea! I shall give you a handsome sum of money to thank you.*

*Zhang Lüer: So you refused! I'd better strangle you after all, with the rope from the Doctor.*

An outrageous demand put in a plausible way! The helpless Old Woman Cai has no alternative but to agree, but Dou'e firmly refuses. Zhang Lüer then tries to kill Dou'e. But his father mistakenly eats the poisoned food and dies. Zhang Lüer greases the hand of the country magistrate and has Dou'e sentenced to death. Now comes again satire from the playwright on corrupted officials. The magistrate drops on his knees in gratitude to the plaintiff, because "every one coming with a case is a source of wealth," "an opportunity to ask both the plaintiff and the defendant for money."

In short, *Snow in Midsummer* is a tragedy. Before she is executed, Dou'e makes three vows before her death to assert her innocence: first, "none of my blood goes to the ground, not a single drop of it, but all will fly up to stain the nine-foot long white streamer on the pole;" second, "a big snowfall" comes in the summer that year, deep enough to bury her body; third, "a severe drought that lasts for three years will hit this area." All the three vows, made in a moving and tragic way, come true within three years, and her case is eventually redressed.

Unlike the pure tragedy of *Snow in Midsummer*, *The Riverside Pavilion* is a comedy and *Lord Guan Goes to the Feast* is a historical drama. The former two exhibit Guan Hanqing's strength in graphically depicting female psychology, while *Lord Guan Goes to the Feast* shows the playwright's skill in illustrating a man's courage. It is about General Guan Yu of the Three-Kingdoms Period, who sails across a river in a storm single-handed to attend a banquet that has been set up as a trap for him. By wits and excellent martial skills, he weathers the storm safe and sound. The tune he chants when crossing the river to the banquet is very famous:

*This great river is a noble sight! / A thousand billows flow eastwards, / A few dozen rowers are with me in this small craft; / I go to no nine-storied dragon-and-phoenix palace, / But a lair, ten thousand feet deep, of tigers and wolves. / A stout fellow is never afraid, / I go to this feast as if to a country fair.*

Guan Yu knows very well what awaits him, "a den of fierce tigers and wolves," but he takes it as nothing more than going to a village martial art competition—what a heroic spirit in the face of danger! Yet, at the torrential river, recalling his campaigning up and down over the last twenty years he can not help but sigh with emotion:

An illustration of *Snow in Midsummer* (*Dou'e Yuan*).

(Saying):

*What a spectacular view!*

(Singing, to the tune of *zhu ma ting*):

*Tossing waves, hill after hill, / Where is young Zhou Yu today? / He has turned to dust. / General Huang Gai suffered much; / The warships that conquered Cao Cao are no more. / But the waves are still warm from past battles— / This wrings my heart!*

(Saying):

*This is no river water,*

(Singing):

*But the blood of heroes / Shed for these twenty years!*

Zhou Yu and Huang Gai were both famous generals in the State of Wu during the Three-Kingdoms Period. Twenty years before, the State of Shu, which Guan Yu served, in collaboration with the State of Wu, defeated the army of the State of Wei led by Cao Cao in the well-known Chibi Campaign. Twenty years had passed and both Zhou Yu and Huang Gai were gone. Yet the war still continued, so the blood of numerous soldiers continued to flow.

A classical Chinese silk painting of the *za ju* of the Song Dynasty.

Because of *Snow in Midsummer*, a "denouncement" tragedy, later generations often focused attention on the playwright's forceful "realistic criticism." This overlooked another feature of his work: being solemn and comical at the same time in a drama. Actually, being solemn and comical at the same time is fundamental to Chinese operas. Chinese operas originated from entertainers' jokes and satire that were meant to amuse audiences alongside singing and dancing. Before *za ju* of Yuan was

A painting of the *za ju* team of the Yuan Dynasty at the Peace Temple of Youli, Shanxi.

born, all opera forms, like those of Tang and Song dynasties, featured jesting and joking. Guan Hanqing inherited this, placing seriousness in humor and humor in seriousness. In this, he was very much like William Shakespeare (1564–1616). Both were unrestrained, releasing in scripts their feelings, mirth, laughter, anger and curses. Meanwhile, solemnity, emotion and gravity are never absent. The ability to be both comic and serious at the same time characterizes most great playwrights. All of them possess a feel for real life and for feelings both familiar and unique. Yuan Opera has a set form, often comprised of a prelude and four acts. The prelude is to lead the story, while the act is set by the modes of ancient Chinese opera music. Guan Hanqing initiated the Yuan Opera mode.

# Wang Shifu

Wang Shifu (whose dates of birth and death are unknown) is also a Yuan Opera playwright, sharing similarities with Guan Hanqing, also being a talented member of a story group. Yet unlike Guan Hanqing's works, his work was more often read than performed on stage. The best known of his works is *Story of the Western Chamber (Xi Xiang Ji)*. Unlike other Yuan Opera dramas, which are fairly simple in form and need less complicated props, *Story of the Western Chamber* takes much more to be staged. Because of this, and also because the popularity of dramatic, martial stories, *Story of the Western Chamber*, being in a subtle and exquisite style with elegant and poetic dialogues, was less popular and far from being a hit during the Yuan Dynasty. However, during the Ming Dynasty scholars discovered its high artistic quality. The status of this play rose continuously until it eventually surpassed Guan Hanqing's works.

*Story of the Western Chamber* is adapted from a Tang-Dynasty story titled *Hui Zhen Ji* about a young male scholar falling in love with a young lady, disregarding the then social norms but eventually deserting her. Zhang Sheng, the hero, is young, gentle, handsome, and proud, very particular about choosing a wife, and at the age of twenty-three has never associated with any women. On an outing, he encounters the seventeen-year-old Oriole (Cui Yingying), a very elegant, intelligent, and pretty girl. Zhang falls in love with her at first sight. With the help of her maidservant, Rose (Hong Niang), Zhang begins to associate with Oriole. Several months later, he leaves for the capital to attend royal examinations in order to get an official position, but he never returns.

*Statue of Cui Yingying*, by Qiu Ying of the Ming Dynasty. The scene of Yingying burning incense and praying under the moon is depicted in the Yuan Opera.

Oriole writes him a letter in which she expresses her worries. Zhang, however, heartlessly breaks off the relations with her, because he believes "such an extraordinary girl will be an evil character once entering a high life, and better be left alone." The author of *Hui Zhen Ji* takes sides with Zhang by glossing over his doing. Yet *Story of the Western Chamber*, adapted from *Hui Zhen Ji*, takes another dimension, turning the story into perfect romance with a happy ending.

The story is set in the Tang Dynasty. The nineteen-year-old Oriole, a young lady from a very high official family, accompanies her mother on a trip escorting her dead father's coffin back to their hometown for burial. As the trip is long and arduous, they stop half way to rest in the western chamber of the Salvation Monastery. Zhang Junrui, a young scholar, happens to visit the temple and is taken aback by her divine beauty and elegant appearance. The young man manages to move into the

An illustration of *Story of the Western Chamber*. Yingying is reading a letter from her lover, and her maid Rose is spying behind a screen.

temple, having only a wall between him and the place where the girl stays. At night, when the girl is burning incense in a worshiping ceremony in the garden, Zhang chants a poem to convey his amorous feelings:

*The moonlight dissolves the night, / Spring's lonely in flowers' shade. / I bask in the moonbeams bright / Wondering, where is the lunar maid?*

Oriole returns a verse to match it, and both are surprised and overjoyed at each other's accomplishment. Later, on another night when Oriole is burning incense to the luminous full moon, Zhang plays his lute to convey a love message. Oriole is indeed intelligent, for she is able to tell every detail in the tune:

*The melody flows in an exhilarating medley of sounds. Now like the clash of cavalry sabers; now soft like flowers dropping into smoothly flowing streams. At one time high like the cry of a crane in a breezy moonlit sky; at another, low like lovers' whispers in a private chamber.*

Sun, the Flying Tiger (Sun Feihu), an army officer in Heqiao, on hearing of Oriole's divine beauty, sends troops over to the Salvation Monastery to take her by force. At this critical moment, Oriole offers to marry anyone who can drive away these soldiers. As her heart has been given to Zhang, she secretly hopes that Zhang will have an idea. Zhang does not let her down, for with the help from his good friend, General Du Que, his former classmate, Sun Feihu's troops are forced to withdraw. However, after the danger has passed, Oriole's mother breaks the promise of marrying her daughter to Zhang. Instead, she forces them into a brother-sister relationship. Oriole no longer trusts her mother, and begins to rebel in her own way.

With the help of Rose, Oriole and Zhang manage a secret meeting. Their night rendezvoux continue for a month before Old Madam Cui, Oriole's mother, finds out. When interrogated, Rose talks "smoothly" to the angry old woman, making her unable to advance any further reproach. At the end of her resources, she asks Zhang to attend the royal examinations, and if he receives officialdom, to come back for a wedding. Luckily, Zhang comes out first of all candidates. Zhang and Oriole are eventually together, just as the old saying goes, "Lovers are destined to marry."

Although literary works describing romantic rendezvous have been many since ancient times, the *Story of the Western Chamber* is unique because it gives the meeting a very poetic and romantic feel. Not only is the lust between the hero and the heroine apparent, their love, feelings and psychological changes are all graphically portrayed. Due to external pressure—indirectly from the feudal ethical code and directly from the Oriole's mother and Old Madam Cui, wife of the late prime minister—their love is full of rebellion. The most fascinating characters in the story

An opera stage of the Yuan Dynasty.

are two young girls, Oriole and her maidservant Rose. Oriole is her own mistress, a courageous young lady with meticulous thinking. When Zhang's situation is unknown, she manages to sound him out. When Zhang misunderstands her intention and bursts into her boudoir, she firmly reproaches him, stopping his blunder in her pride as the daughter of the prime minister. In their relationship, she is, to some degree, not passive. Rose, after the *Story of the Western Chamber,* has become a synonym for matchmakers.

*Story of the Western Chamber* is written in a very flowery language. The author was good at adapting lines from predecessors' poems. The best known is the following:

*The cloudy sky frowns gray / Over the yellow-bloom-paved way. / The western breeze does bitterly blow, / As north to south the wild geese go. / Like a wine-flushed face are the leaves so red, / Dyed in the tears that parting lovers shed.*

The second line is adapted from a verse by a Song-dynasty poet, Fan Zhongyan, yet Wang Shifu changed "the yellow-leaves-paved way" to "the yellow-bloom-paved way" in order to portray the sad feeling of tearful Oriole when parting with Zhang before the latter leaves for royal examinations in the capital. Many lines in classical Chinese lyrics are associated with yellow blooms. Probably the most famous are *ci* poems by Li Qingzhao:

*Say not my soul / Is not consumed. Should the west wind uproll / The curtain of my bower, / You'll see a face thinner than a yellow flower.*

*Listening to Music*, by Wang Shuhui, a painting of a scene from *Story of the Western Chamber*.

and another one, "A Weary Song to a Slow Sad Tune" by the same author:

*All over the ground are the yellow flowers, / When emancipated, / No one comes to pick up even one.*

The "yellow flower" is a metaphor for Oriole's emaciated appearance, also mirroring her sadness. It refers to chrysanthemum blooming in late autumn when the weather has turned fairly cold from early snow or frost. For this reason, chrysanthemum is viewed as "a real gentleman among all plants," a popular symbol for lofty virtues started by Qu Yuan, a poet in ancient China. Qu Yuan described himself thus: "At morn, I drink the magnolia's dripping dews, / At nightfall, I on asters' fallen petals dine." Tao Yuanming, a poet of the Eastern Jin Dynasty, wrote the famous lines, "While picking asters 'neath the Eastern fence, / My gaze upon the Southern mountain rests." In his secluded life, Tao Yuanming took chrysanthemums as his friends, refusing to yield to the authorities for food. Yuan Zhen, the author of *Hui Zhen Ji*, exclaimed, "After chrysanthemum, no more flowers to bloom!" All of these literary masters spoke highly of the yellow flower from a spiritual perspective. The yellow flowers in the *Story of the Western Chamber* serve a double purpose: to symbolize Oriole's sadness when parting with Zhang, and as a token of her unyielding personality.

# Classical Fiction in the Ming Dynasty

*Romance of the Three Kingdoms,*
*Outlaws of the Marsh* and *Journey*
*to the West*

*Decameron*, written by the Italian Giovanni Boccaccio during the fourteenth century, contains historical events, legends and stories. The hero in *Gargantua and Pantagruel* written by Francois Rabelais was also a well-known character in French folklore. In China, also during the fourteenth and fifteenth centuries, fictions (*xiao shuo*) about historical romance and folk tales came into being.

*Romance of the Three Kingdoms*, the earliest novel in China, appeared in the late Yuan or early Ming period, authored by Luo Guanzhong. Its stories are based on historical facts and judgments from a history book entitled *Recordings of the Three Kingdoms* by Chen Shou of the Jin Dynasty, as well as on notes made by Pei Songzhi of the Southern Dynasty. Promptbooks and drama scripts from Song and Yuan were probably also involved. *Romance of the Three Kingdoms* is viewed as a novel extended from historical romance and tales. After its publication, it was printed again and again with many changes. The earliest known edition of the book is one printed during the first year of the Jiaqing Period of Ming (1522), titled *Popular Story of the Three Kingdoms* in twenty-four volumes, each containing ten chapters. During the reign of Kangxi, in the Qing Dynasty, Mao Lun and Mao Zonggang, father and son, revised the book's chapters, plots and language, making the story more complete and smooth to read, eventually producing the final 120-chapter edition that we have today. The fiction has different chapters called "*hui*," and each *hui* has couplets as its title. This became the form used by all later Chinese classical novels. The evolution of the novel from historical facts and tales was a common one that could be found in

*Xiao shuo*
This refers to a kind of fiction in Chinese, and first appeared in *Zhuangzi*, meaning chatter of no significant consequence (*A Brief History of Chinese Fiction*, by Lu Xun). During the Qin Dynasty and the two Han Dynasties that followed, *xiao shuo* meant nothing but small talk on streets or markets, often short and frivolous in content and far from the literary form now known as a "novel" that appeared later. *Xiao shuo* as a literary form has its roots in myth, religious legends, tales and fables found in the works of ancient philosophers. To many people, Chinese fiction in a true sense began during the Tang Dynasty.

*Along the River at Qingming Festival* (detail), by noted painter Zhang Zeduan of the Northern Song Dynasty, collection of the Palace Museum, Beijing. The development of city economics in the Song Dynasty promoted the flourishing of urban culture. The novel genre exists and develops at this time.

all later classical novels. The story *Outlaws of the Marsh* has been popular since the Southern Song Dynasty, and Song Jiang, the hero of the story, did exist in history. Some of the contents of *Records of Xuanhe Period, Song Dynasty,* a popular book for storytellers, as well as some Yuan plays and folk stories during the Song and Yuan dynasties were sources for *Outlaws of the Marsh.* Another book, *Tripitaka's Search for Buddhist Sutras,* was the predecessor to *Journey to the West.* Most Chinese fiction evolved from historical stories, and structurally speaking, they were nothing more than simple string of different events. Evaluated by rigid Western criteria, which can very demanding about structures and rhythms, these stories may receive a negative judgment. However, early Chinese fiction is not without literary significance.

Urban development brought a thriving entertainment industry.

Stories told in markets were different, such as "Jiang Shi," telling historical stories or "Pu Dao Gang Bang," telling stories about heroes' fights. The sources for these stories were citizen literature in an early form. In the narrow and small spaces in a city, people loved to escape daily life through stories. They loved stories about heroes or supernatural beings, while the world in which these stories were set (known as *jiang hu*), full of outlaws, risks and uncertainty, was becoming more developed. Although in many cases *jiang hu* overlapped with a real, historical setting, part of it would be totally different, like the marsh of Liangshan Marsh. Figures in this alternative, fictional society were ordinary people, peddlers or small government officials, yet they observed laws entirely different from those in our world.

# Romance of the Three Kingdoms

*Romance of the Three Kingdoms,* authored by Luo Guanzhong (c. 1330–1400), describes political and military struggles that lasted more than ninety years between the late Eastern Han and the Western Jin Dynasty (169–265). The story contains many of the values and beliefs that prevailed in that period. The beginning verse chants:

*The world under heaven, after a long period of division, tends to unite; / After a long period of union, tends to divide!*

This belief meets common Chinese historical philosophy: situations cycle every five hundred years. The period of the Three Kingdoms is a chaotic era in which heroes and capable people of various kinds rose and vied for a position. Intense power struggles make up much of the novel's fascinating plot. The strategies utilised by the protagonists are numerous and twisting: "beauty trap," "self-torture scheme," "turn the enemy's agent against him," "fight by fire or water," and so forth.

*Romance of the Three Kingdoms* has three matchless characters: Zhuge Liang, the epitome of wisdom, Guan Yu, the symbol of loyalty and righteousness and Cao Cao, the treacherous pretender. By the time Luo Guanzhong wrote this novel, late Yuan or early Ming, popular judgment about the characters of the Three Kingdoms Period were entrenched, and storytellers during the Song Dynasty exhibited a clear liking for Liu Bei and a dislike of Cao Cao. Much earlier, the Tang-Dynasty poet Du Fu wrote the following verse to express his esteem for Zhuge Liang:

*Being visited twice and then often conferred on affairs of statecraft, / In installing and promoting up two reigns as their adamantine support, / You in person the state's corps dispatch lead, but died before triumph could be won. / It doth make all our heroes mourn your noble cause with tears.*

In keeping with Confucianism, Zhuge Liang accomplished doctrines like "in a humble position, keep virtuous; in a prominent position, mind the suffering of the broad masses."

*Attending Thrice and the Final Meeting*, by Sun Yi of the Qing Dynasty, collection of Tokyo Museum of Japan. This painting takes its theme from the story of Liu Bei attending Zhuge Liang's cottage three times and finally inviting him out from the mountains.

He maintained an easy state of mind when living a secluded life, when in a high position, "bending his back to a task until his death." Meanwhile, Guan Yu was equally admirable. He was righteous and loyal, possessing invincible martial prowess. Many stories about him have been told with much relish throughout history, including "Guan Yu rides on a solitary journey," "Guan Yu, single handed, goes to a feast set up as a trap" and "having a scraped-bone surgery." Unlike unscrupulous heroes in other popular stories who may visit brothels, abuse alcohol or pick fistfights, Guan Yu has an impeccable character. Both Zhuge Liang and Guan Yu, as described in the novel, have highly admirable wisdom and prowess and are free from the defects of ordinary people. This preference is partially attributable to the author's belief that Liu Bei represented the orthodox branch of the Han royal family. By elevating and magnifying the virtues

Guan Yu is shot by a toxic arrow. The famous doctor Hua Tuo cures him by scraping the poison from his bone. Guan Yu remains talking and laughing as if nothing had happened. Displaying uncommonly heroic spirit, Guan Yu plays *go* and drinks wine while Hua Tuo treats him.

of Liu Bei, the author presented us with the image of a military counselor with wonderful foresight. Meanwhile, Cao Cao was put down as an evil minister, distorting what he really was in history.

As the Three Kingdoms Period really existed in Chinese history, and the stories about the Three Kingdoms had come down in history through storytellers' books, *Romance of the Three Kingdoms,* just like *Outlaws of the Marsh* and *Journey to the West*, is well known to almost every family in China. Taking the novel as a history book, readers often take the characters in the novel as real ones in history. Because of the novel's tremendous popularity,

Zhuge Liang is very witty and sly. He intimidates the army of Sima Yi with an empty city and the stratagem of presenting a bold front to conceal a weak defence becomes the most brilliant stratagem in *Romance of the Three Kingdoms*. This stratagem is widely talked about in history and Zhuge Liang is used to denote wit in Chinese.

some critics warned that the novel was just "seventy percent true and easily misleading." Zhuge Liang's stories, for example, had historical basis, yet the novel described him being witty and foresighted to the point of a supernatural being. One of his deeds was to anger Zhou Yu, the military governor of the State of Wu three times, making the latter die from vomiting blood. In history, Zhou Yu did not actually die from jealousy of Zhuge Liang's exploits. The author added embellishment when describing their wisdom pitted against each other.

*Romance of the Three Kingdoms* tells a story of an era when heroes rose to compete chaotically with one another for the upper hand. It is set in a panoramic background, its story told in a highly spirited way, and through characterization publicizes Confucian doctrines about politics and human behavior, the author's yearning for a rule of benevolence, mutual assistance, honor and trust as well as other traditional virtues. By taking sides with Liu Bei and putting down Cao Cao, the author was actually denouncing, though in a round-about way, the rule of the Yuan Dynasty. However, even the hero has no power to retrieve what has been lost. In the end, the loyal Zhuge Liang, the epitome of Confucian spirit, dies before a triumph is won.

# Outlaws of the Marsh

Historic stories and stories about heroes' fights during the Song Dynasty gave birth to the chapter-titled fiction *Outlaws of the Marsh*, authored by Shi Nai'an (c. 1296–1370), written very close to the completion of *Romance of the Three Kingdoms*.

Most of the characters in the story gathered in Liangshan Marsh, a fictional place of "jiang hu." Readers of one generation after another took these characters as heroes simply because they held the banner of "acting in the name of heaven." Lu Zhishen and Wu Song, two of them, do help the weak out of difficulties. They, together with other heroes characterized in the novel, live a quite free life, eating and drinking luxuriously – just as ordinary readers longed to do. The friendship among the men described in the novel is moving, being willing to go through fire and water together.

Plots in the novel are highly dramatic, such as "Wu Song, drunk, beats Gate Guard Jiang," "Capture birthday gifts by a ruse," "Sagacious Lu makes a shambles of Wild Boar Forest," "Lin Chong shelters from a snowstorm in the mountain," "Wu Song kills a tiger with bare hands," "Blood pool in the Mandarin Duck Tavern," "Three attacks at the Zhu Family Manor," all full of thrill and suspension. Fairly simple in structure, the fiction evolves along a single thread around one character, and the chapters about him, if put together, make a fine biographical sketch and can pass as an independent story.

The characters in the novel come from very complicated backgrounds, some being land or property owners, some bandits, some officials of high position, and some just vagrants shifting from place to place. They gather in mountains with a sense of acting in the

A painting of *Outlaws of the Marsh* by Shi Nai'an, by Yan Shaoxiang.

*Wu Song Fighting the Tiger*, a painting from an *Outlaws of the Marsh* story by Liu Jiyou.

name of heaven and a strong material desire. They fear "neither heaven, earth nor the court, sharing gold and silver together and clad in rare silk, eat meat and drink wine to their fill." They take action to uphold justice yet they kill people indiscriminately. For instance, in the section "Blood pool in the Mandarin Duck Tavern," Wu Song kills fifteen people before he stops, only three of them being his enemies. Another character, Li Kui, in the part "Snatch a victim from the execution ground," chops many people to death with his "two axes flying up and down." Some contemporary scholars have viewed this as an indifference to human life. Yet, if we take into consideration the source of the novel, storytellers' promptbooks, we may ascribe these bloody descriptions as intended to cater to the "blood lust" of listeners,

A New Year picture, *Three Attacks at the Zhu Family Manor*, of the Qing Dynasty.

a common strategy storytellers use to grab attention. We can see the trace of this blood lust in *Decameron, Gargantua and Pantagruel* and in horror films today.

As a scholar, while adapting the novel from popular stories, Shi Nai'an could not help embedding in it feelings and values of his own. Luo Guanzhong gave much emphasis to orthodox Han thinking, while Shi Nai'an pictured a scholars' dream as being to "establish exploits." Under his brush, the characters only do things in the name of heaven, never trying to take supreme power. All they ask is to be accepted by heaven and to serve it. In the end, after pledging submission to the court and being granted amnesty, these heroes led by Song Jiang set off to battle other rebellions. This ending mirrored the author's longing for achieving great deeds for the court. This is why during the Cultural Revolution in China in the 1970s, some critics denounced the novel as a rebellion-surrender story against only corrupt officials, not the supreme ruler—the emperor. This denouncement is probably a fair endorsement of the purpose of the author. Yet the author's dream did not last long, as all the heroes in the book expire, leaving later generations to pass their own judgment.

## *Journey to the West*

The Chinese nation has a history of five thousand years. *The Book of Songs* has much description of war and expeditions, farming in different seasons and amazing phenomena. The inclination for dramatic plots peaked during the Han and Tang dynasties and then took a turn to stillness, in Song-Dynasty scholar literature. The famous classics *Romance of the Three Kingdoms, Outlaws of the Marsh* and *Journey to the West*, all experienced a "snowballing process," from storytellers' promptbooks to finalization by scholars. All of them contain "human characteristics," particularly *Journey to the West.* The hero of this book is a fearless monkey able to perform supernatural feats. After he becomes a Buddhist he escorts his master, Monk Sanzang, on a pilgrimage to the west seeking Buddhist scriptures, a trip full of trials and tribulations. Only the courage and power of his disciples, mainly the Monkey, save the master from man-eating devils - eighty-one times in total. This absorbing story is full of imagination. The first seven chapters describe the Monkey, an irresistibly charming character with a defiant and fearless personality, raising havoc in heaven before he is imprisoned by Buddha.

The Monkey is born out of a magic stone, and learns magic arts like riding his cloud and changing into seventy-two forms. He is quick-witted and resourceful, each hair on him is able to change into a different thing, and each somersault he makes covers a distance of five thousand kilometers. He styles himself as the king of the Flower and Fruit Mount, he grabs by force a weapon from a palace under the sea; he makes a big disturbance in the netherworld until he receives "amnesty" from the supreme ruler of heaven, and is granted the title "protector of horses." Yet the Monkey soon finds out that this is just a very insignificant position, he storms out of the heaven's palace in anger and returns to his Flower and Fruit Mount. The next time, the Jade Emperor gives him the title "great sage equaling the heaven." The Monkey is pleased, for he believes from then on he is an equal to all gods, even to the Jade Emperor. However, when the Queen Mother is holding a "banquet of peaches," all the immortals are invited but not him. The Monkey finally comes to the realization that the equality he believes he has is just a fantasy. The angry Monkey breaks into the Jade Pool where the banquet is to be held, and by creating sleeping insects he makes everyone there fall sound asleep, leaving all wine and food for him. After he eats and drinks to his fill, he staggers and sways, charging his way, by mistake, to Tushita Heavenly Palace where Lord Laozi of the Great Monad reigns. He then eats all the golden eternal pills he finds there. The angry Lord Li, after capturing him, tries to burn him in his stove. The Monkey survives the trial of burning and is left with a pair of "fire eyes and gold pupils." The helpless Jade Emperor, finally, asks the Buddha for help. The Buddha subdues the Monkey by turning his palm into a huge mountain and placing it on the Monkey. Five hundred years later, on his trip to the west to seek scriptures, Xuanzang, the Monk from Tang, frees the Monkey from under the mountain. From then on, the

A portrait of Wu Cheng'en.

*Raising Havoc in Heaven*, by Liu Jiyou, depicting the battling scenes of Sun Wukong and the heavenly soldiers.

Monkey follows the monk, saves his life repeatedly and escorts him all the way to the west.

Raising havoc in heaven is like a mischievous deed by a naughty boy, unrestrained and hearty. He is eager to prove his status and power, not to control the freedom and life of other people, but his own power, and the power of creation. He can pull out his hairs and change them into any form he wants.

*Journey to the West* is largely a fairy tale about gods, devils and super-natural beings, and this is seen clearly in the characterization. The "Great Sage of Equal to the Heaven" is clearly a monkey; lively, witty and mischievous. His partner, the Pig, styled as "Martial from the Heaven," is fat, lazy and always hungry for food. He is stubborn and sometimes stupid. Another name of his is the "Pig of Eight Abstinence," suggesting the rules of Buddhism—abstinence from killing, stealing, sexual lust, nonsense talk, drinking alcohol, sitting or sleeping on luxurious seats or beds, using make-up and eating non-vegetable foods. Yet in the story, contrary to the meaning his name suggests, the Pig indulges in all of them! The Pig has some clever tricks, yet all of them fail before the Monkey. The two characters are not opposing each other, just showing different sides of human nature. If we had only the wisdom seen in *Romance of the Three Kingdoms*, without the mischievousness seen in *Journey to the West*, or, if we had only the moving brotherhood among men as seen in *Outlaws of the Marsh*, but without romantic experiences as seen in *A Dream of the Red Mansions*, it would be a sad world.

Most of the evil spirits the Monkey encounters when he raises havoc in the heaven, as well as on his trip to the west, come from the spirits of animals in various forms: ox, goat, horse, deer, elephant, tiger, leopard, fox, mouse and scorpion on the ground, eagle in the heaven, and dragon, turtles, crabs and shrimps in water, plus the monkeys in the Flower and Fruit Mount, lions in the Leopard Mount, and oxen in the Bull Hill. All of these animals preserve their original nature, represented from a child's perspective, but with careful observation and a lively imagination.

The journey to the west to seek Buddhist sutras by Xuanzang (600–664), the Monk of Tang, is a very important event in Chinese history. In order to seek the ultimate truth of Buddhism,

A stage photo of the TV play *Journey to the West*.

the monk Xuanzang set off alone from Chang'an (present-day Xi'an) to India on AD 629, the third year of the Zhenguan Period during the reign of Emperor Taizong. He followed the West River Corridor, out of the Yumen Pass, through Xinjiang, and, passing over a hundred states, eventually arrived in India where he stayed for a dozen or more years. He returned to Chang'an in AD 645. In history, he was a brave and courageous person, yet in the novel, he is described having too many worries, soft but kind-hearted. The reason for this is probably the change in his status. The leading role is not him but the Monkey. It is against his soft nature and muddle-headed behaviors that the courage and brave deeds of the Monkey become prominent. The story must, of course, be read as a fairy tale about a versatile and smart monkey rather than as record of the arduous west-bound trip made by Xuanzang for sutras.

# Strange Tales from a Chinese Studio

## Short Stories of the Qing Dynasty

*Strange Tales from a Chinese Studio*, written by Pu Songling (1640–1715), a well-known literary man of the Qing Dynasty, is an excellent collection of short stories from ancient China. It is generally believed that the stories were written after Pu had traveled to southern China and were not compiled into a book until the eighteenth year of the reign of Emperor Kangxi (1679). It took about forty years for the author to complete the final version. Therefore, it is not restricted to a limited time or area. As an extensive and heterogeneous book including 500 stories,

A portrait of Pu Songling.

*Strange Tales* is unavoidably a mixed work of masterpieces and less successful pieces. Nevertheless, the body of the work is fascinating. *Strange Tales* is praised as a pinnacle of classical Chinese fiction.

Pu Songling was born into a declining gentry family during the period of transition from the Ming Dynasty to the Qing Dynasty. The characters such as "son of an aristocratic family of long history," which frequently appear in the book, are more or less autobiographical. Pu had an intellectual pedigree, with many forebears excelling in the imperial examinations and ascending to official rank. But his father failed in those examinations, and had to give up scholarly pursuit and engage in trade. During the chaotic dynastic transition from Ming to Qing, constant wars ravaged the country. Pu's family, with many children to feed, fell into decline and became even poorer when Pu was born. A bright and diligent boy, Pu made himself known when he was nineteen, ranking first in three consecutive examinations at the county, municipal and provincial levels, after which he failed repeatedly. Nevertheless, he did not give up seeking scholarly honor and the consequent official positions. Having struggled for almost his entire life, Pu was finally recommended to the court as a scholar, soon after which he died. Having talent but never the chance to use it, Pu spent his life in destitution and frustration. He served as assistant to some officials and later became a teacher at a private school to earn a living, before he settled down as a tutor to the sons of a powerful man named Bi. He stayed in Bi's

*The Cricket* depicts the story of a common family contributing a cricket to the royal court. Collection of the National Museum of China.

house for thirty to forty years, almost until his death. A tutor's life involved no more than reading, writing and teaching. It also provided him a chance to meet people from the scholar-bureaucratic class. Local celebrities, officials and men of letters were among his acquaintances. Although he did not make it in the imperial exams, he was not without admirers. But even as he associated with some scholar-bureaucrats, he was obviously living in poor and humble situations. He yearned for the life of a scholar-bureaucrat, but he also had concern and sympathy for the lower class, including scholars who failed to rise in the world.

Pu's personal experiences and sensibilities largely determine the content and themes of his works. The Studio is the study room where Pu read, wrote and taught, while Strange Tales, as Lu Xun noted, are "stories of immortals, ghosts, and demons." The stories can roughly be divided into the following categories: romances between talented young scholars and beautiful women; stories of friendship between human and human, human and non-human (such as foxes, beasts and ghosts); rebellious stories that show discontent over social injustice; allegories that satirize human vices.

The first category — romances between talented young scholars and beautiful women such as *Yingning, Fox-Girl Qingfeng, Lian Suo, Lian Cheng* and *Daughter of Revered Mr. Lu* — account for the greatest proportion and are most captivating to the audience. Such stories usually feature a talented young scholar, who, in his lonely long days occupied by studying, comes across a beautiful young woman transformed from a ghost or vixen spirit and falls in love instantly before they are separated for various reasons. Having been through all kinds of hardships, the lovers are finally reunited. Some scholars argue that this could be Pu's own fantasy regarding his own solitude. As a family tutor, Pu spent a good part of his life separated from his wife and children in an official's house. He might have dreamed about romances that could not be. So he created stories about were-foxes and ghosts for solace. It is worth noting that although the stories have similar plots, the characters are colorful and diversified. Yingning's innocence, Qingfeng's shyness and Lian Suo's talent impress the reader deeply. As ghosts, they are not ghostly, but "humane and kind," incarnating ideal women and ideal love for the author. Beautiful and intelligent, kind and sweet, faithful and passionate, they have every feminine virtue and choose their lovers by character and talent rather than family background. More crucially, in the pursuit of happiness, they are willing to make sacrifices and overcome one obstacle after another until united with their lovers at the end.

The second category consists of stories about friendship between human and human or human and non-human, such as *Scholar Ye, Tian Qilang, Jiaona* and *The Snake-Charmer*. These stories vary in style and content. For many researchers, *Scholar Ye* is a semi-autobiographic story that mirrors Pu's own experiences. It also has to do with repaying the help of a superior who appreciates Ye's talents. *Tian Qilang*, however, is about reciprocating the help given by a friend. *Jiaona* involves love, but there is also the theme of friendship, which is different from the love between husband and wife. *The Snake-Charmer* tells a story of dear friendship and deep sympathy between human and snake, snake and snake, which serves as a sharp contrast to the inconsistency of human relationships.

The third category, rebellious stories such as *Xi Fangping, A Dream of Wolves, Hong Yu* and *Shang Sanguan*, are mostly about ghosts but bear references to social context. They can be divided into two subcategories: one criticizes the corrupted court and the rich and the powerful that dominate society. The common people who are wronged deeply can only resort to extreme means or the power of ghosts or sacrifice to achieve justice. For example, in *Xi Fangping*, Xi's father offends a rich and powerful

*Painted Skin* depicts the story of a ghost who disguises himself as a beautiful girl under a painted skin and eats humans. Collection of the National Museum of China.

man called Mr. Yang, who greases the palm of officials in the lower world and puts the old man into hell. Xi throws himself down there to plead for his father, only to find himself tortured by the officials who have taken bribes from Mr. Yang. He makes an appeal and then resorts to an even higher authority, but fails again and again. This story, although it describes what happens in the lower world, is obviously an allusion to the social injustice of the day. *A Dream of Wolves* reveals the brutal nature of the feudal officials. *Hong Yu* tells how a fox called Hong Yu helps her lover punish villains. *Shang Sanguan* is a story about a woman who is ready to sacrifice her life to avenge the evil. The other subcategory, including *The Imperial Examiner, Jia Fengzhi, Wang Zi'an,* and *Sequel to the "Yellow Millet Dream"* expose the evils and corruptions of the imperial examination system and convey the frustration and disappointment of those who failed to rise through it. Such stories are often satirical. For example, *The Imperial Examiner* and *Jia Fengzhi* make fun of the silly officials who are in charge of the imperial examinations, while *Wang Zi'an* and *Sequel to the "Yellow Millet Dream"* reveal the pathetic situation of the scholars who fail in the examinations repeatedly, even in their dreams, and could only sigh "Alas! Glory and wealth can only be found in castles in the air and ocean bazaars," as concluded in *The Raksasas and the Ocean Bazaar.*

The fourth category, such as *A Taoist in Mount Lao, Painted Skin, Cursing the Duck* and *Rain of Coins*, are allegories that satirize human vices. With a strong moral, these stories get their message across through humor. *A Taoist in Mount Lao* ridicules those who get petty profit before they become insatiable and bump "into the wall" and fall "loudly to the ground." *Painted Skin* scorns foolish people who are blinded by their lust.

The consideration of themes and content does not explain fully the status of *Strange Tales* as an artistic pinnacle in the history of ancient Chinese literature. Ancient Chinese fiction could generally be divided into two groups: one in classical Chinese and the other in vernacular Chinese. Fiction was only in classical Chinese, the best part of which were short stories, before the Song Dynasty, except for a few preserved in the *Bianwen* (Buddhist classics in the form of ballads and stories) of Dunhuang, whose language was close to vernacular. The origin of classical Chinese fiction could be dated back to the Pre-Qin era, when some myths, tales and fables were pregnant with certain ideas, such as sections and chapters in *The Book of Mountains and Seas* and the fables in *Zhuangzi*. During the Wei, Jin, Southern and Northern dynasties, sketches that described individuals or strange happenings were popular and collected into books such as *Anecdotes About Spirits and Immortals, The Record of the Nether World* and *Collection of*

*Anecdotes.* With fairly complete plots, some portrayal of characters and more sophisticated language, these works were still too true to be called fiction, and the authors lacked the self-awareness of artistic creation. In fact, these strange tales were records of something real to the audiences of the day. In the history of Chinese literature, fiction in its true sense did not appear until "Chuanqi" (prose romances) of the Tang Dynasty were created. One of the significant signs of the birth of fiction is, as Lu Xun pointed out, "the intention to create fiction." In other words, as opposed to records of real people and real happenings in the Wei and Jin dynasties, these tales are subjective writings, with the plot, the characters, the language, and the themes becoming more sophisticated and relevant. In the Song Dynasty works in vernacular Chinese appeared. From then on, classical Chinese fiction and vernacular Chinese fiction began to develop in parallel.

*Strange Tales*, which "uses prose romances to record strange happenings," as Lu Xun puts it, is a pinnacle of classical Chinese fiction. It inherits and develops the artistic tradition of the records of the Six Dynasties and the prose romances of the Tang Dynasty. In terms of themes and content, it is mostly about ghosts, inherited from the tradition of the records of the Six Dynasties. However, a major development is that Pu clearly realizes that his work is fiction, while the records of the Six Dynasties are believed to be factual accounts. It is the "idea of imaginative creation" that helps the author break through the fetters of facts, give a full play of his creativity and convey strong feelings through his works. At the same time, *Strange Tales*

**Prose romance**
as a literary form rose after the records of human anecdotes and supernatural happenings made by Wei and Jin scholars, and was at a peak during mid-Tang, with a wide range of subject matters, romances, gallant deeds, historical happenings, and association with supernatural beings in dreams. It can be said that the rising of romances signifies the maturity of prose romance as a literary genre. Tang prose romances, often flowery in language, complicated in plot, complete in structure, and sharp in characterization, mark the maturity of Chinese short stories as a literary genre.

The former residence of Pu Songling.

inherits the complete structure from the prose romances of the Tang Dynasty and the "Huaben" (promptbook stories) of the Song and Yuan dynasties, but shows far more ingenuity in terms of plot design. Furthermore, compared to the rather crude portrayal of characters in the prose romances of the Tang Dynasty, it makes significant artistic achievement, especially in the depiction of ghost-girls who are different from humans but have the virtues and dispositions of women in this world. In particular, there is generally a short comment by "the Chronicler of the Tales" at the end of every story, carrying on the mode of expression Sima Qian uses in *Records of the Historian*. The comments of "the Chronicler of the Tale" are often thoughts and feelings on life and fate or advice and warnings to the audiences. Therefore, more than just "tales," the stories about foxes and ghosts mirror the experiences of the author and the realities of the wider society. Those incredible stories of ghosts contain a kernel of truth; the light-hearted ridicule and mockery mask serious thoughts on life.

Once published, *Strange Tales* became very popular. Many writers followed suit in later generations, bringing prose romances to a revival during the mid-Qing Dynasty. But these works are nothing compared to *Strange Tales*, which has remained popular with people today. Many stories from the book have been adapted for plays, movies and even soap operas, reaching wider audiences. It has been translated into over twenty foreign languages and has since been read by people around the world.

# A Dream of Red Mansions

## The Pinnacle of Classical
## Literature

Since *The Book of Songs,* Chinese literature has continuously produced female characters, including legendary beauties and chivalrous girls such as Hua Mulan, who disguises herself as a man to join the army in place of her ailing father. "Stories of Exemplary Women" in the historical records of every dynasty are accounts of what women have done—but this is no more than giving up their lives after their husband dies or killing themselves to preserve their "chastity," and their names are not clear in these records. The idea that women have no value of their own became more prevalent at a later stage, when women were often treated with distain and made a scapegoat. Female characters in fiction from this time are detestable: the fiery and ferocious Mrs. Gu "the She-Tiger" in *Outlaws of the Marsh,* the female characters who are slaves to their lust in *Jin Ping Mei* (or *Plum in the Golden Vase*), and the concubine named Da Ji who brings calamity to the country and its people in *Creation of the Gods.*

Then, *A Dream of Red Mansions* seemed to be born out of nowhere during "the Golden Age" of the reign of Emperor Kangxi and Emperor Qianlong. The self-worth, the freewill, the talent, the yearnings, the great joys and sorrows of women were suddenly revealed, sometimes in torrents of vivid, intense prose, sometimes in simple, restrained but loaded language. The author expresses his admiration for women directly through the voice of the characters, in particular the hero Jia Baoyu, who says, "Girls are made of water, men of mud. I feel clean and refreshed when I'm with girls but find men dirty and stinking," which has become a well-known saying in China. The author sympathizes with women who are oppressed by the

A portrait of Cao Xueqin, by Jiang Zhaohe.

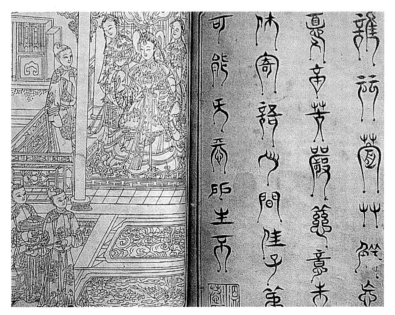

An illustration of *A Dream of Red Mansions*. The Cheng Jia edition includes the first eighty chapters by Cao Xueqin and the other forty chapters by Gao E.

patriarchal society. Moreover, as a writer leading a precarious life, how could he not identify with the disadvantaged group called "women"that share his feelings and fate?

Originally known as *The Tale of the Stone*, this full-length novel could be summarized in one sentence: *The false becomes true when the true is taken for false / Nonbeing begins to be where being is nil.* Cao Xueqin did not finish this work but only wrote eighty chapters, for he had put so much energy and heart to it that he "died as his tears dried." A man named Gao E continued what he had left and wrote the last forty chapters before it was published as *A Dream*. There are twists and turns in the first eighty chapters, yet the story develops in a rather easy and smooth way; while the last forty chapters are full of violent ups and downs, and the characters often come to their end in an unexpected way. Compared to the first eighty chapters, which are subtle or tempered, the last forty chapters are bold and unrestrained, reflecting the more explicit attitude of the latter author.

A *Dream* puts women on the center stage, with the "Twelve Beauties of Jin Ling" as its principal characters. In Chapter Five, Jia Baoyu, the hero in the novel, visits the "Illusory Land of Great Void" in his dream and sees "the records of the past and future of all girls," where there are no names but poems that predict their fate. The records consist of "First Register of Twelve Beauties of Jinling," "Second Register of Twelve Beauties of Jinling" and so on. The "Twelve Beauties" in the First Register live in the great house of Jia, with the Grand View Garden as their quarter.

Arguably the first full-length Chinese novel about a great noble clan, *A Dream* tells the tragic story of how the powerful Jia family meets its doom. Two of the grandfathers in the family established themselves by military exploits and were granted titles of the highest nobility: the Duke of Ningguo and the Duke of Rongguo. At the time of the third generation described in the novel, the family produces no worthy offspring and lives on what their ancestors have left. Jia Jing, the eldest male member in this generation who is "so wrapped up in Taoism that he takes no interest in anything but distilling elixirs," is obsessed with the idea of becoming immortal. His eldest son Jia Zhen, to whom he has relinquished his title, takes no interest in studying and "lives for pleasure." Sleeping with his daughter-in-law and toying with pleasure boys and young girls together with his sons, this patriarch of the mansions of Ning and Rong leads a rotten life. Lady Dowager Shi, wife to the eldest son of the Duke of Rongguo, is the only person survivng from the second generation of the family. She dotes on Jia Baoyu and is always a harbor of refuge for him. Her two sons are the "backbone" of the third generation: the elder one Jia She inherits the title; the younger one Jia Zheng is regarded as the most "decent" man in the two mansions.

The love story between Jia Zheng's elder son, Jia Baoyu and his cousin Lin Daiyu serves as the main thread of the novel. The feudal ethical code puts pressure, sometimes visible and sometimes invisible, on young men and women in a noble family, who cannot express their love openly or seek freedom of marriage. The story ends with Daiyu's death and Baoyu becoming a monk. As a tragedy, *A Dream* is full of tension, with all kinds of human feelings such as joy, sorrow and anger vividly depicted. Day-to-day life in the Grand View Garden, mundane scenes such as drinking, eating crabs, making poems and telling jokes are described in detail. Always telling what happens as it is, the author seldom assumes any moral authority to condemn the evil, while he clearly shows respect for the talented but ill-fated girls living in the Grand View Garden.

*Alas for her wifely virtue, / Her wit to sing of willow-flowers, poor maid! / Buried in snow the broken golden hairpin / And hanging in the wood the belt of jade.*

The above poem noticed by Baoyu in "the Illusory Land of Great Void" in his dream is full of metaphors, with the golden hairpin designating Xue Baochai (also cousin to Baoyu) and the jade designating Daiyu. The fact that the destiny of the two most important female characters is predicted in the same "verdict" meris some analysis.

According to *Stories of Exemplary Women* in *The Book of Later Han*, a man named Yue Yangzi misses his wife (note that she has no name) so much that he discontinues his study and goes back home. The woman stops her loom, cuts the cloth in half and tells him that the pursuit of scholarly honor is like making cloth in that all one's previous effort would become wasted if one gives up halfway. Awakened to his error, the husband goes back to continue his study. And the woman has become a paragon of "wifely virtue," that is, being able to restrain oneself

*The Grand View Garden* (detail), by painter of the Qing Dynasty. Collection of the National Museum of China.

and regarding the success of one's husband as one's priority in life. A prudent girl with an even disposition, Baochai recognizes and accepts the established social order. For her, it is the only choice for Baoyu to become "a respectable official" and serve for "the betterment of society," and with her talents, character and vision, she could surely help him one day. In this sense, Baochai has the "wifely virtue." When she first comes to the Jia mansion and meets Baoyu, Baochai is just thirteen years old. "A beautiful, dainty girl of great natural refinement," she is on the waiting list for the court and escorted by her family to the capital, lodging in the Jia mansion. She might be chosen to become a lady-in-waiting or companion to a princess. The outcome of the selection is left unknown, Baochai settles down in the Jia mansion and wins the favor of the Lady Dowager and Lady Wang (Baoyu's mother), and is even liked by Lin Daiyu and Shi Xiangyun, cousin to Baoyu. However, the true love of Baoyu is always Daiyu. For Baochai, Baoyu is probably not an ideal man to marry, because he would not be subject to the established order, which is the ultimate difference between him and Baochai, although his rebellious acts are often ineffective against the powerful system. In the last part of the novel, Baoyu loses his jade and becomes mentally deranged, and his family wed him to Baochai. By the time he recovers, what is done cannot be undone. He later takes the imperial examinations to appease his family and comes out quite well. Nevertheless, he eventually leaves home and goes to a monastery, fulfilling a seemingly farfetched promise he makes when Daiyu is alive, whereas Baochai is fated to be deserted by her husband as "the broken golden hairpin" "buried in snow."

Although not perfect in the eyes of Baochai, Baoyu still has quite a few merits. For example, compared to her brother Xue Pan, the "most vicious ruffian alive" who is "extravagant in his habits and insolent in his speech," the respect and consideration for women shown by Baoyu is precious. Furthermore, the male characters in the novel hardly deserve the "wifely virtues" of Baochai. Even Jia Zheng, the man with the best reputation in the clan, who is "so fond of studying since a child" and "well-disposed to scholars and, like his grandfather before him, delighted in honoring worthy men of letters and helping those in distress," is careless and incapable, even silly. The author's scorn for Jia Zheng is often veiled and suppressed. For example, Jia Zheng is "known for his fine method of schooling his sons and disciplining his household," but he seems to have no better way to educate his sons than waving sticks and yelling "you young rascal" at them. As for the other young men in this extended family, he is even less able to guide or control them. Besides, he is "too easy-going to take mundane matters seriously, preferring to give all his leisure to reading and chess," which makes Xue Pan even weaker. He is also very considerate towards Jia Yucun, who tries a case unjustly and helps Xue Pan get away with murder.

"Her wit to sing of willow-flowers, poor maid" conveys the author's sympathy towards Daiyu, who has talent but no opportunity to use it. Xie Daoyun, a female poet in the Eastern Jin Dynasty, once was asked to complete a couplet. As the first line is "To what shall I compare snow so fair?" Her cousin declaimed "salt scattered everywhere," while she declaimed "soft willow-flowers dancing in the air," which is far better in terms of artistic conception. And she was known to have the "wit to sing of willow-flowers" from then on. Just like Xie, Lin Daiyu has a quick poetic mind and refined taste. When other sisters rack their brains for good lines, she seems confident and carefree. When the time is up, beautiful verses that eclipse all the others just flow out of her pen. Gifted girls such as Daiyu, Baochai, Jia Tanchun (Baoyu's half sister), and Shi Xiangyun start a Begonia Club with Baoyu, nicknamed "Much Ado About Nothing," and hold several poetry festivals that might be called "carnivals" for people living in the Grand View Garden. Writing poems about begonias and chrysanthemums, they are actually showing their talents and expressing their aspirations. Daiyu's poem about the begonia reads:

*Half-rolled the bamboo blind, half-closed the door, / Crushed ice serves as mould for jade pots. / Some whiteness from the pear-blossom is stolen, / Some of its spirit winter-plum allots.*

And she questions the chrysanthemum in her poem:

*Proud recluse, with what hermit are you taking refuge? / All flowers must bloom, what makes you bloom so late?*

These lines exhibit her talent and taste, making her first in the poetry competition. The spirit of Daiyu echoes that of a group of Chinese scholar-hermits who are intelligent and upright, but not made for this world. In her poem on the chrysanthemum she makes a direct reference to Tao Yuanming, the famous poet who resigned office to lead a humble farmer's life, seeking spiritual freedom. She therefore has the deepest and most natural empathy for Baoyu, who hates the idea of becoming a slave of bureaucracy. She seems also not to care much about material pleasures. She lives in the Bamboo Lodge, where there is "a narrow pebbled path flanked with bamboos" and "the ground on either side of it was carpeted with dark moss." It is not a magnificent house, but quiet, elegant, and charming, with books scenting the air. There are "brushes and inkstone on the desk by the window," and a bookcase "piled with books," as described in

*Night Banquet at Yihong House*, by a painter of the Qing Dynasty, represents the birthday party of Baoyu with his girl friends in *A Dream of Red Mansions*.

the novel. It looks like a place of a scholar with good taste rather than that of an ordinary girl engaged in needlework.

A refined young lady, Daiyu does not have a happy life. With her mother dead, she goes to visit her grandma, the Lady Dowager, before her father dies too. She is loved dearly by her grandma and becomes close to her cousin Baoyu at first sight, which gives her some comfort. But life for an orphan under the roof of an extended noble family is not easy. Being an intelligent and sensitive girl, she often feels as if treading on thin ice, as she puts in the poem:

*Each year for three hundred and sixty days, / The cutting wind and biting frost contend. / How long can beauty flower fresh and fair? / In a single day wind can whirl it to its end.*

*Eating Crabs at Ouxiang House*, a New Year picture of Yangliuqing, Tianjin, collection of the Russian Geographic Society.

Aware of the proprieties within a noble family and afraid that she would be derided for walking away, she goes no further than observing the world around her and keeping her feelings and thoughts to herself. She does not intend to win favors from the senior members or to form friendship with her peers. On the contrary, with a sharp tongue, she sometimes offends others. Both outsiders who come for shelter and understand the complicated politics involved, Baochai and Daiyu take quite different approaches. One tries her best to adapt and obey, while the other just follows her heart. The two girls have different family backgrounds too. Baochai's uncle is a high official in the capital before he gets promoted to take a provincial position, which has an effect on the mentality of the two girls and also becomes an important factor for the Jia family when they consider whom Baoyu should marry. Generally speaking, Baochai manages to be part of the established family and social order, while Daiyu tries to keep spiritual freedom. However, neither of the two comes to a happy ending.

Another principal female character in the novel is Shi Xiangyun, a girl neither sentimental nor sophisticated, neither a cynic, nor a follower of the crowd, but natural, spontaneous and big-hearted, often drunk with the raptures of life. In Chapter Sixty-Two, the author describes how Xiangyun gets drunk after drinking games and sleeps tipsily among peonies. "She was sound asleep and covered with peony petals, which had floated over from all sides to scatter, red and fragrant, over her face and clothes," as he puts it, "bees and butterflies were buzzing and flitting around her." The female characters in the novel are often talented and pure, but they are for most of the part shackled by conventions. It is only Shi who gets chances to disregard decorum. Her spirit is reflected in the lines she writes: "Leaping and rushing, / The river's waves surge towards the sky," while her destiny is predicted in the lines: "The river Xiang runs dry, / the clouds over

Chu have flown," which suggests that her situation is not totally hopeless.

There are also a few keen-witted and capable female characters in the novel. Wang Xifeng, daughter-in-law of Jia She, is a vigorous and shrewd woman. As put in Chapter Two, she is "extremely good-looking and a clever talker, so resourceful and astute that not a man in ten thousand is a match for her." Although illiterate, Xifeng has great executive ability and a quick mind that outshines her peers, which is shown when she helps to keep house for the Rong clan. With a nimble tongue, she is good at amusing people with jokes and becomes a pet of the Lady Dowager, the paramount authority

*Constructing a Poem on a Storm on a Stormy Night,* an illustration of *A Dream of Red Mansions.*

in the family. Jia Tanchun, half sister to Baoyu, has comparable executive ability and literary talent as well, but no selfish motives. "So talented and high-minded, / She is born too late for luck to come her way," as described in Chapter Five.

With lesser character and talents, the daughters of Jia are almost eclipsed by Daiyu, Baochai, Xiangyun, and Xifeng. Jia Yingchun, daughter of Jia She and his concubine, stays in the house of her uncle Jia Zheng for a few peaceful years, before she is forced to marry a police commissioner called Sun Shaozu. She is practically sold to Sun by his father, who has borrowed five thousand taels from him, and is soon tortured to death by her husband. Xichun, another daughter in Jia's family is good at drawing and later becomes a nun, sleeping "by the dimly lit old shrine."

*A Dream* is a tragedy of "the gentler sex." Daiyu dies of blood-vomiting; Baochai ends up virtually a lonely widow; Tanchun marries far away from home and no one knows what happens to her; Xifeng spends so much energy on scheming and plotting that she gets sick and is disliked by her husband and finally dies in depression. The tragic endings of these characters reflect the author's philosophy of life.

As a monumental work surpassing the ancients and amazing contemporaries, *A Dream* was created during the Kangxi, Yongzheng and Qianlong periods, when Chinese feudalism was still in its heyday. The author Cao Xueqin was born into a distinguished family. His great grandfather served as Textile Commissioner of Jiangning Prectecture (present-day Nanjing and six contiguous counties) and his family played host four times to Emperor Kangxi on his itinerant trips south in Nanjing, which suggests the close relationship between the emperor and the family. Cao was born in 1715, almost the end of the era of Kangxi.

The royal visits brought Cao's family honor and fame, but the large-scale construction work carried out to accommodate the emperor and his escort also pulled it deeply into debt, whence crises were rooted. During the first year of the reign of Yongzheng when Cao was eight years old, his grand-uncle Li Xu's property was seized by the court, implicating the Cao family, whose wealth was also confiscated the fifth year of Yongzheng. With a vague memory of a life of extravagance, Cao heard many tales coming down through generations of the past glory. Therefore, the ostentation and luxury of an extended noble family described in *A Dream* is not wholly imagined by the author but based on life. It is because of this that the novel can be read as an encyclopedia on the life of the Chinese upper class during the mid-eighteenth century.

The author of *A Dream* intends to challenge many things, but first and foremost romance novels popular during the Ming and Qing dynasties. These works are "largely nothing more than stories about secret affairs and elopement, without expressing any true heart of men and women," criticizes the author. "They are always about those stereotyped romantic figures, described roughly together with some of their poems and other works. As for the details such as food and drink in everyday life, there is no account at all." Cao writes about "true heart" and everyday "food and drink," which indeed differentiates his works from all the others. Cao also makes critical observations on the established opinions about women, the widely acknowledged responsibility of man to win scholarly honor and then serve for the betterment of society, and traditional Confucian ideas. There were at the time many new trends of thought that affected Cao deeply. Figures such as Gu Yanwu, Huang Zongxi, Wang Fuzhi, and Li Zhi were challenging, even undermining traditions.

However, behind all this is the author's great compassion and disillusion. His experiences as a son born to a distinguished noble family that had seen its fortune fall and the sharp contrast between the affluence of his childhood and the poverty of his adult years lead to a more penetrative perception of the vanity of life. As he puts in the poem:

*All men long to be immortals, / Yet to riches and rank each aspires; / The great ones of old, where are they now? / Their graves are a mass of briars.*

*All men long to be immortals, / Yet silver and gold they prize, / And grub for money all their lives, / Till death seals up their eyes.*

*All men long to be immortals, / Yet dote on the wives they've wed, / Who swear to love their husband ever more, / But remarry as soon as he's dead.*

A still from the television play *A Dream of Red Mansions*.

*All men long to be immortals, / Yet with getting sons won't have done. / Although fond parents are legion, / Who ever saw a really filial son?*

Riches and status written in water, scholarly fame and official positions nothing solid, children not dependable, all the boom and bustle just the past—Cao sees through the superficiality of life, but he is still full of fire. "Every word is written with life blood," "Pages full of fantastic talk / Penned with bitter tears / All men call the author mad / None his message hears," as he puts in the novel. As a great humanist, he even finds something agreeable or likable in the "villains" and shows consideration for their wrongdoings—even if they are subject to human weaknesses—although he is not without values or judgments. Moreover, living in a time when literary inquisition prevailed, he has to be careful

Cao Xueqin Museum in Huangye Village, Fragrant Hills, Beijing.

to avoid harm, which is why he does not make much explicit judgment in the novel. Cao, also known as Mengruan, was described by his friends as "turning a cold shoulder to others" and as "prouder than Ruan Bubing," who was a scholar during the dynasties of Wei and Jin. Ruan Bubing, whose formal name was Ruan Ji, would turn a cold shoulder to those he did not like, and was very cautious when he wrote anything. "He intended to remonstrate and ridicule, while his prose is usually obscure and difficult to understand." Writing *A Dream*, Cao is similar to Ruan in that he has to take great pains to mask his intentions, which are in part to remonstrate and ridicule. As a result, later generations have various readings of the novel, and "Redology" (the study of *A Dream*) is comparable to the study of Shakespearean works.

# Lu Xun

## Founder of New Vernacular Literature

# The Transformation of Literature

The *Youth Magazine* (renamed *New Youth* from volume two) started its publication on September 15, 1915 in Shanghai. The birth of this magazine officially opened the modern "New Culture Movement" in China. With *New Youth* as the center, a large group of new-style intellectuals gathered together. Holding high the two banners of "science" and "democracy," they launched a cultural enlightenment campaign lashing out at the feudalism that had lasted for the past several thousand years in China. This storm of movement explicitly demonstrated two directions at the outset, destruction and construction, namely, fighting against old morality and old literature and promoting new morality and new vernacular literature, with the former primarily attacking Chinese feudal thought and feudal ethical codes and reassessing the value of traditional culture, and the latter introducing into China trends of thoughts prevailing in the West, such as equality and freedom, personality liberation, and social evolutionism to direct the construction of new morality and new vernacular literature.

A literature revolution soon started along with the development of the "New Culture Movement." In January 1917, *New Youth* (No. 5, Vol. 2) published an article

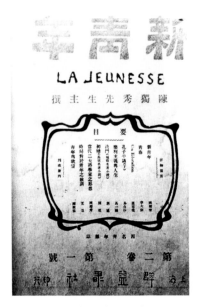

*New Youth* was the major base for promoting "New Culture" and "New Vernacular Literature."

Hu Shi—a representative of the "New Culture Movement."

by Hu Shi (1891–1962) "A Modest Proposal on Literature Reform," bringing forward "eight proposals" for literature reform in connection with the current conditions in traditional Chinese literature. As a matter of fact, Hu Shi's views were all directed towards one core problem. He believed that one era should be marked with the literature that belonged to that era. When the old era came to an end, the writings in classical Chinese that voiced old literature had lost their vigor. In a new age, a

Chen Duxiu

new language tool should take its place and this new language tool was writings in vernacular Chinese. This showed Hu Shi's stress on the change of the linguistic form of literature. Soon after this, Chen Duxiu (1879–1942) published his "On Literature Revolution" (No. 6, Vol. 2) to give a response and, holding high the banner of "Revolutionary Literature Army," declared war on the thousand-year-old feudal literature. He took Hu Shi's "eight proposals" as the pioneer for literature revolution and put forward "Three Principles" in literature as the content and path to follow for literature revolution, namely, "Down with the aristocratic literature that is ornate and adulatory and build literature for the people that is familiar and lyrical," "Down with classical literature that is trite and grandiose and build realistic literature that is fresh and sincere," and "Down with mountain and forest literature that is involved and abstruse and build social literature that is popular." Hu Shi's and Chen Duxiu's viewpoints on literature revolution were enthusiastically met by many new-style intellectuals. Qian Xuantong (1887–1939) and Liu Bannong (1891–1934) published numerous articles to justify the trend that writings in classical Chinese would be replaced by writings in the vernacular. Fu Sinian (1896–1950), Luo Jialun (1897–1969) and others started to publish *New Trend. New Trend, New Youth* and *Weekly Review,* which was started some time afterward, constituted the effort to promote new vernacular literature. On this basis, extensive discussions on how to build new vernacular literature were held.

Zhou Zuoren

In December 1918, Zhou Zuoren (1885–1967) published *People-Oriented Literature* (*New Youth,* No. 6, Vol. 5), stating that new vernacular literature is "people-oriented literature." Zhou Zuoren expressed his view in the article as follows: The nature of literature is the rediscovery of the "people" and the basic objective of literature is to "promote a healthy and all-round development of human nature." New vernacular literature must show concern for people's real life and the real society, and reflect the "non-human life" of the common people at the bottom of society in particular. In addition, study, examine and analyze "various problems of life" from the perspectives of social plight and people's predicament and then open up an "ideal life" so as to reshape the people and the society through literature.

The idea of "discovery of people" was in fact based on humanism that originated from the West and its direct theoretical source was from the humanist literary theory of the Shirakaba School that was very popular in Japan. Humanism, a cultural theory that had played a significant role in the development of European literature in the nineteenth century, was transplanted indirectly into China by Zhou Zuoren to serve as the theoretical construction of China's new vernacular literature, making the revolutionary elements in the content of literature more specific. In his article "Commoners" Literature" (*Weekly Review,* No. 5, 1919), published a month later, Zhou Zuoren, guided by humanism, further brought forward the idea of "commoners'

literature." As a concrete embodiment of "people-oriented literature," "commoners' literature" faithfully advocated writing about "the real conditions of the common people" in popular vernacular Chinese, truthfully reflecting "the joys and sorrows, successes and failures of ordinary men and women," and honestly writing out "the true thought and facts" of most people. Zhou Zuoren's views on literature intensified and supplemented the idea of revolution in literature content promoted by Chen Duxiu and his peers. Summing up the content of new vernacular literature with the term "people-oriented literature" was a concrete embodiment in terms of content in the construction of new vernacular literature, wherein a new pattern of new vernacular literature involving the content conveyed, objects described and significance and orientations in literature was established.

And, what is more, the ultimate aim of rediscovering and showing concern for the "people" in new vernacular literature was to reshape the "national character," which, in Lu Xun's words, was to "bring to light pains so as to arouse the attention for treatment and rescue." At the beginning of modern Chinese literature, Lu Xun and Zhou Zuoren were the first who brought forward and promoted the modern literature idea of reshaping "national character." In principle, this literature idea gave expression to the substantive characteristics of modern Chinese literature, and its main spirit ran through the entire course of modern Chinese literature.

The impact of the literature revolution was immense, and brought about the transformation of Chinese literature at this historical juncture. This transformation was omni-directional, including literature ideas, literature content and literature language, and even the relationship between Chinese literature and world literature. To be more specific, the ideas that "literature is to convey the Tao" and "literature is to expound the ideas of the sages" gave way to the ideas that "literature should be people-oriented"and "literature should center on life." In content, new literature completely criticizes and rejects feudal ideology and culture, highlights the significance of literature in real life; instead of writing about "emperors and ministers" and "handsome scholars and pretty girls," commonplace and unremarkable laborers and intellectuals become the primary heroes and heroines in literature; in literature language, vernacular Chinese replaces the classical Chinese; in its relationship with world

"New Vernacular Literature" during the "May 4th" Movement started with Lu Xun's appeal to "save the children." *Rescue the Young* (1918), an illustration of Lu Xun's essay by painter Qiu Sha.

literature, conservativeness and isolation give way to using and absorbing rich traditions from world literature. From this time, the traditional literature that had lasted for several thousand years in China declined, and a new period of modern Chinese literature unfolded.

# Lu Xun

Lu Xun was the greatest thinker and writer of the twentieth century in China. On September 25, 1881, Lu Xun was born into a

Lu Xun

large family in Shaoxing, Zhejiang. He grew up under the influence of traditional culture and folk culture from an early age. While pursuing his studies in Nanjing and Japan, he had extensive exposure to Western culture. After having experienced the tremendous changes in China's society, thoughts, and culture that had started at the end of the ninteenth century, he gradually developed his own independent thinking. Beginning with the publication of his first essay "The History of People" in 1907 and publishing *A Madman's Diary*, the first short story written in vernacular Chinese in China, in *New Youth* in May 1918, he wrote a great number of works. His major works include collections of short stories, *Call to Arms, Wandering, Old Tales Retold*, a collection of prose poems, *Wild Grass*, a collection of essays, *Dawn Blossoms Plucked at Dusk*, and sixteen miscellaneous works including *Hot Air, Grave, The Canopy, Two Hearts, False Liberty*, and *Essays of Qiejieting* and some others. Apart from these works, Lu Xun also wrote some academic works such as *A Brief History of Chinese Fiction* and *An Outline of the History of the Han Dynasty Literature*. Reshaping "national character" is not only Lu Xu's viewpoint on literature, but also a major subject matter in his literary creation. *The True Story of Ah Q*, the most representative work of Lu Xun's stories, is a typical example of his taking apart the Chinese people's personality and a concentrated embodiment of his thought on reshaping the Chinese people's "national character."

In *The True Story of Ah Q*, Lu Xun created the figure of a typical Chinese peasant from the old feudal society, Ah Q, a proletarian at the bottom of society as well as a backward peasant with deep-rooted feudal thought without being aware of it. The most outstanding characteristic of Ah Q is his method of winning moral victory. Instead of facing up to the defeats and insults he confronts in real life, Ah Q goes after moral victory and the self-satisfaction brought about by this victory through spiritual self-deception. He can flaunt past achievements that have never existed and false visions that will never happen in the future to relieve himself of his real embarrassment and worries. Though he never finds out who he really is, he can claim that "We used to be much better off than you!" Though he has no wife, he says, "My son will be much better off in the future." When beaten, he consoles himself

A still from the film *The True Story of Ah Q*. Yan Shunkai plays the part of Ah Q.

by taking it as a son has beaten his father or converting defeat into victory by beating himself. When finding it impossible to turn defeat into victory through the method of winning moral victory, he leaves all the insults he has come across behind him by forgetting them, and takes it as if nothing has happened to him after waking up from a sleep. Ah Q's method of winning moral victory is a psychic abnormal state, a narcotic drug that paralyzes the soul of the Chinese people. Ah Q himself and his method of winning moral victory make up a mirror. By creating the image of Ah Q, Lu Xun "reveals the weaknesses of the Chinese people," enabling readers to feel as if he is writing about the readers themselves and at the same time also writing about everyone, opening up a road for introspection. In the subsequent short stories he wrote, such as *The New Year's Sacrifice*, *Medicine*, *Storm in a Teacup*, *My Old Home* and others, Lu Xun exerted

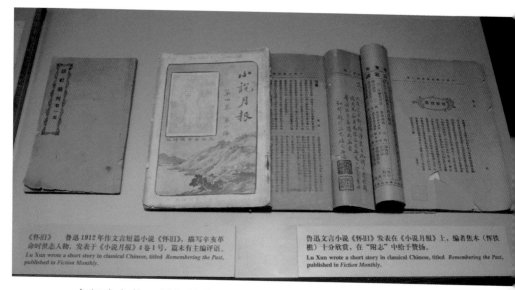

《怀旧》 鲁迅1912年作文言短篇小说《怀旧》，描写辛亥革命时世态人物，发表于《小说月报》4卷1号，篇末有主编评语。
Lu Xun wrote a short story in classical Chinese, titled *Remembering the Past*, published in *Fiction Monthly*.

鲁迅文言小说《怀旧》发表在《小说月报》上，编者焦木（恽铁樵）十分欣赏，在"附志"中给予赞扬。
Lu Xun wrote a short story in classical Chinese, titled *Remembering the Past*, published in *Fiction Monthly*.

A story by Lu Xun published in *Fiction Monthly*, housed in the Lu Xun Museum, Beijing.

himself depicting the ignorance and numbness of the general population and thereby exposed and repudiated the social cause that had created this personality—the feudal system and feudal ethical codes that had lasted for several thousand years.

In May, 1918, Lu Xun's *A Madman's Diary* was published in *New Youth* (No. 5, Vol. 4). *A Madman's Diary* discloses the evil practice of "eating people" in feudal society and is a fierce attack on feudal thought and culture. It is the first mature short story written in vernacular Chinese in the history of modern Chinese literature. Lu Xun continued to put into practice the anti-feudal theme in his subsequent realistic short-story writing in different ways and on different levels. Most of the short stories written during the "May 4th" Movement by Lu Xun were included in his two collections of short stories, *Call to Arms* (1923) and *Wandering* (1926). In writing these two collections of short stories, Lu Xun broke the stereotype and tried many different approaches to writing modern short stories. Modern Chinese short stories started and matured from Lu Xun and became the major source of development of various forms of modern Chinese fiction.

Lu Xun was both a pioneer and a founder of modern Chinese literature. It can be argued that Lu Xun's contribution to modern Chinese culture is no less than Shakespeare's contribution to Western culture.

# Modern Fiction

## Echo of the Times

# Mao Dun and Modern Fiction

During the "May 4th Movement," with the publication of Lu Xun's short story *A Madman's Diary*, various attempts were made in the new vernacular fiction in terms of subject matters, themes, expression, and even length. By the 1930s, novels and novellas had become extremely noteworthy for their extensive coverage of society and history.

Mao Dun

In 1933, Mao Dun's *Midnight* was published, which marked that the modern Chinese novel had come to real maturity. Mao Dun (1896–1981), formerly known as Shen Dehong, style name Yanbing, was born into a literary family in Tongxiang County, Zhejiang, in the late Qing Dynasty. In his childhood, he was exposed to, and influenced by, traditional Chinese culture. Mao Dun's major works include a trilogy, "The Erosion" (*Disillusion, Indecision, Pursuit*), *Rainbow*, *Midnight*, and *Frosty Leaves are Redder than the Flowers of Early Spring*, a novella, *The Shop of the Lin Family*, and a collection of short stories, "A Village Trilogy" (*Spring Silkworms, Autumn Harvest, The Last Days of Winter*).

*Midnight* is the representative work of Mao Dun's novels. Taking a figure of the national bourgeoisie, Wu Sunfu's, history of struggle as the main plot, *Midnight* presents a panoramic view of the vast and grandiose social context of the 1930s and the people active at that time and offers a profound analysis of the intricate and complicated class relations involved. This includes contradictions between the national bourgeoisie and imperialism, the comprador bourgeoisie, the governing class, the working class, and the peasant class. Wu Sunfu ended in failure, symptomatic of the decline of the bourgeoisie. In this novel, Mao Dun suggested that the capitalist path would not work in semi-colonial and semi-feudal China. He used this conclusion to give a response to the debate on the social nature of China that was being conducted among cultural circles at the time.

In *Midnight,* many characters are portrayed against the social context of the day, among which the tragic hero Wu Sunfu is the most successful. Wu Sunfu possesses the great aspiration of promoting national industry and Chinese operation capacity. He is not only equipped with advanced managerial experience acquired from his overseas studies in European countries and the United States, he also has a strong personality and is self-confident. Even so, under the joint attacks of imperialism and the bourgeoisie, Wu Sunfu has no choice but to impute his pressure to his workers, and eventually ends with failure. Though doomed to failure, he still fights defiantly against pressures from multiple sides, which gives him a hue of solemn and tragic color. In addition, Wu Sunfu is a successful paradigm

茅盾的长篇小说《子夜》(原名《夕阳》) 手稿

Manuscript of the novel *Midnight*, housed in the Modern Chinese Literature Museum.

of the characterization of typical characters under typical environments. In characterization, Mao Dun gives a lot more prominence to class and social context. Therefore, each character in the novel is a representative or a model of the social class to which they belong. Both an individual person and a typical representative of the national bourgeoisie, Wu Sunfu has the dual nature of a revolutionary character and the apathy of the national bourgeoisie. In the social context of semi-colonial and semi-feudal China, Wu Sunfu's failure is the failure of the class for which he stands. This failure suggests that the capitalist path is not the right choice for the national bourgeoisie.

The epic features displayed in *Midnight* in mirroring the panorama and development of the age reveal Mao Dun's deep thought. Meanwhile, creating typical characters by means of typical environments and the narrative technique of revealing

A still from *Spring Silkworms*, a film adapted from the novel of the same title by Mao Dun.

social contradictions through rational analysis, as practiced by Mao Dun, forms the basis for many Chinese novels. A large number of analytical novels reflecting social, political, and economic structures and contradictions came out after the publication of *Midnight*. By the late 1930s, the tradition started by Mao Dun in realistic novel writing had gradually become the mainstream and peaked in the 1950s and 1960s.

# Ba Jin and His "Torrent Trilogy"

Anti-feudalism is the overall trend as well as the major subject in modern Chinese literature. Ever since Lu Xun, the anti-feudalism subject has been given constant attention by the new vernacular literature writers. But the work that has expanded the subject of anti-feudalism in breadth and depth is the "Torrent Trilogy" by Ba Jin. Ba Jin (1904–2005), formerly known as Li Yaotang, was born into a bureaucratic landlord's family in Chengdu, Sichuan. He witnessed conflicts of interest within an extended feudal family, and how his elder brother became the victim of the extended feudal family. Ba Jin's life experiences in his early years, and his anarchist and humanistic thoughts

Ba Jin

once he grew up, prompted him to criticize feudalism. While he was studying in France in 1927, Ba Jin wrote his first novelette *Destruction*, and started his literary career as a writer. Ba Jin's major works include "Torrent Trilogy," "Love Trilogy" (*Mist, Rain, Lightening*), *Garden of Repose, Ward No. 4* and *Cold Night*.

"Torrent Trilogy" is about the rise and decline of an extended feudal family. It includes three novels, *Family* (1931), *Spring* (1938) and *Autumn* (1940). It completely pulls apart the hypocritical mask of feudal autocracy and the feudal family system, makes public the bloody slaughter and sins behind the mask, proclaims that the feudal system is doomed to die, and calls on all young people to rise up in rebellion. Of the three novels, *Family* is the one that has attained the highest literary achievement. *Family* mainly tells about the love tragedies in the Gao's family. Juexin, the eldest son of the Gao family, and Qian Meifen (Cousin Mei) have been in love since childhood. But Cousin Mei's mother turns down Juexin's marriage proposal and has Cousin Mei married to another man without much thought. She does so just because she has had a dispute with Juexin's stepmother over the game table. Cousin Mei became a widow one year after marriage and before long dies in loneliness and desperation. Ruijue is Juexin's wife. Juexin, after losing Cousin Mei, regains some emotional comfort from his wife Ruijue, but happy days do not last long. When Ruijue is about to go into labor, the old master of the Gao's drives her out of the house and sends her to the countryside for the delivery with the excuse of avoiding bloodshed and fatal disaster, which eventually causes her death from difficult childbirth. The love affair of Juehui, the third young master of the Gao's, and the servant girl Mingfeng is also a tragic love story, which is destined to bear no fruit in such a family. Upon learning that she will be made concubine of Feng Leshan, an official more than sixty years old living in retirement, Mingfeng commits suicide by throwing herself into a lake. Juehui left his home with indignation, and this brings the end of the novel. *Spring* and *Autumn* are the continuation of the Gao's story, telling about the tragedies and struggles of the younger generation, which has contributed to the fall of this big feudal family.

The characterization of Juexin, the eldest son of this big feudal family, is a success. Juexin has become a classic figure in the history of modern Chinese literature. Juexin is the outcome of the alternation of the old and the new societies. He has acquired

A still from *Family*, a film adapted from the novel of the same title by Ba Jin.

the ideal personality of a faithful follower of the feudal ethical codes and has also gone through the baptism of the "May 4<sup>th</sup>" Movement. After the death of his father, he, as the eldest son and eldest grandson, assumes responsibility for the big feudal family. Though he is fully aware that the feudal family and feudal ethical codes have ruined his youth and happiness and feels much sympathy for his brothers' rebellion, his filial duty and responsibility for the feudal family have shackled him in the depth of his soul. In order to hold together superficial harmony in the big family, he has to make up with the seniors and juniors and make concessions, which eventually results in his cowardly character. But his compromises fail to bring harmony in the family; on the contrary, it ruins the happiness he and Cousin Mei should have and kills Ruijue. Juexin is both the victim of the old family system and the vindicator of the old family ethics. This echoes Lu Xun's view as expressed in his *A Madman's Diary*, that the ones that get eaten by people also eat people. And, what is more, Juexin is well aware of this point. Clear-headed in mind and cowardly in action, he experiences severe anguish, but he is incapable of rising up in rebellion.

Third brother Juehui is completely different from Juexin. Juehui is an idealistic and passionate new youth. Fearless, rebellious, he dares to go back on his feudal parents' authority and detests all injustices and oppressions, but at the same time he is timid and weak-willed and naïve, and in his mind the new life in the future is just an indistinct vision. Just because of this, Juehui is real. He is not only a real individual, but also a symbol of the "May 4$^{th}$" youths. He embodies the dauntless courage and forever-going-forward passion of the youths of the time. In this sense, *Family* is a significant novel that reflects the "May 4$^{th}$" spirit of the time. The rebellious acts of the "May 4$^{th}$" youths have eventually awakened thousands upon thousands of "Juehuis" and inspired them to move on forward boldly for the sake of freedom and ideals.

# Lao She and "Beijing Style" Citizen Fiction

In the 1930s, *Camel Xiangzi* by Lao She enjoyed equal popularity with *Midnight* by Mao Dun and *Family* by Ba Jin. These three novels made up the three pinnacles of modern Chinese fiction creation. Lao She (1899–1966), formerly known as Shu Qingchun, a Manchu, was born into a poor family in Beijing and grew up among the urban residents in the middle and lower echelons of society. For most of his life, Lao She was in the teaching profession, from a schoolmaster to a middle school teacher to a university professor. His teaching experience in London University (1924–1929) had a far-reaching impact on his literary creation. In connection with Western culture,

Lao She

he started to examine traditional Chinese culture and began writing novels. His representative works include the novels *Lao Zhang's Philosophy, Two Ma's, A Tale of the Cat City, Divorce, Camel Xiangzi, Four Generations Living under One Roof,* novellas, *Crescent Moon, This Life of Mine,* and a short story, *The Soul-Slaying Spear.* Lao She also wrote some excellent plays after 1949. *Dragon Beard Ditch* and *Teahouse* are the best-known of his plays.

*Camel Xiangzi,* one of Lao She's major novels, has enjoyed worldwide popularity. It gives a vivid portrayal of the tribulations of a rickshaw man, Xiangzi, a man living in the lower social stratum of Beijing.

Xiangzi is a young farmer who has wandered to the big city to earn a living. The greatest goal in his life is to have a wife and children, have food and clothing, and live a stable and smooth life. He is determined to work hard and make enough money to buy a rickshaw of his own through pulling rickshaw. Yet his chances of realizing this modest wish are very slim under the gloomy social conditions of the time. The first rickshaw he buys is stolen by a wounded soldier. On another occasion, after he has made enough money and is ready to buy another rickshaw, his money is extorted by Detective Sun. He has to sell his third rickshaw because he does not have money for his wife's funeral. Xiangzi's experiences break his dreams time and again and eventually defeat him. Xiangzi, though originally full of hope for life and the future, starts to give in to self-indulgence, intoxicating himself with

A *hutong* in Beijing.

smoking and drinking and cheating. When he finally finds out that his beloved Xiaofuzi has hanged herself, he breaks down and becomes a walking ghost, more dead than alive. The tragedy of Xiangzi voices the author's criticism of society as well as his reflection on human nature. Xiangzi's adversity stems from social conditions. A corrupt and disordered society is unable to guarantee even a basic living environment for the ordinary people. No matter how hard he tries, Xiangzi can never get adequate food and clothing. His moral degeneration is also a humanistic tragedy. In the beginning, Xiangzi is a man of a good character, self-reliant and confident in himself. But when his dream is shattered, he goes to extremes with ease. He knows how to make an effort for a good living and how to bring himself to destruction. He gambles; he is lazy, crafty; he plays dirty tricks, comes to blows with others, profits from others' expenses, and even risks his life for sixty silver dollars. The distortion of human nature caused by social conditions and Xiangzi's frailty of spirit are vividly portrayed.

Apart from following closely the adversities of the urban residents at the lower layer of society, Lao She also critically examined and reflected on traditional Chinese culture through portraying old-style Beijing citizens. Moreover, Lao She's fiction is marked by a strong local cultural features. Through drawing heavily on the spoken language and the refined and processed Beijing dialect, with which he was familiar, Lao She sketched out numerous lifelike metropolis hand scrolls mirroring the life of Beijing people. It can be concluded that the strong local features expressed in his fiction added a new style to modern Chinese literature—"Beijing Style" fiction, which has had a far-reaching influence on the fiction and drama creation of the writers who came after him.

# "Beijing School" and "Shanghai School"

As a phenomenon in modern Chinese literature, the terms "Beijing School" and "Shanghai School" came directly from a controversy between Beijing writers and Shanghai writers in the 1930s. The "Beijing School" refers to a group of liberal writers active in Beijing or cities around Beijing in North China, who shared similar literary values. Most "Beijing School" writers looked at society and life from the perspectives of tradition and country life, attached more importance to the aesthetic value of literature itself, and opposed political utilitarian purposes and the commercialization of literature. The "Shanghai School" includes a wider range of writers. Generally speaking, most of the "Shanghai School" writers examine life from the urban people's point of view, and their works are closer to commercial literature and pop literature.

The most important writer of the "Beijing School" is Shen Congwen. Shen Congwen (1902–1988), formerly known as Shen Yuehuan, was born into a prestigious military family in Fenghuang County, Hunan. Fenghuang County is located at the intersection of Hunan, Sichuan and Guizhou provinces in the Yuanshui River drainage area, where the Dong, Miao and Tujia ethnic groups live. Upon graduation from primary school, Shen Congwen joined the local army and moved around the Yuanshui River area with the troops. During this period, he became acquainted with life and local conditions in this multinational region and accumulated a lot of life experience and source materials for literary creation. By the time he made a name for himself, Shen Congwen still clung to his "countryman" identity, and continued to create lots of unique literary works from the perspective of a "countryman." His major works include

Shen Congwen

the novels and novellas *Longzhu, Border Town, Long River*, the collections of short stories *Fringed with Flowers, Eight Running Horses, The Old and the New, Housewives, The Spring Lantern*, and collections of prose writings, *A Biography of Shen Congwen, Random Notes from Hunan*, and *Western Hunan*.

*Border Town* is Shen Congwen's most important work. In this novella, Shen Congwen creates an ideal countryside by the name of Western Hunan, and the story is set against a small border town called Chadong in this Western Hunan. Cuicui, the heroine of the story, lives an idyllic life in Chadong with her grandfather, an old boatman. Shunshun, the owner of the boats, has two sons, Tianbao and Nuosong, who both fall in love with Cuicui. But Cuicui loves Nuosong. In order to help his younger brother and Cuicui to fill their wish, Tianbao sails away from home alone to make a living, but dies in an accident. After losing his brother, Nuosong is tormented with self-reproach and guilt and finally leaves Cuicui and the small town. Before long, the old boatman dies a sudden death. Cuicui is left alone and

Fenghuang County, western Hunan Province.

starts her endless waiting for the return of Nuosong. Nuosong "probably will never return, or he will be back tomorrow." The story comes to an abrupt end with Cuicui's waiting. This is a tragic love story. Cuicui, Tianbao and Nuosong are faultless, but they are fooled by fate that is beyond their control. The story presents a tragic color of ancient Greek tragedies, but the love tragedy of Cuicui is not Shen Congwen's primarily concern. What Shen Congwen praises profusely through this tragic love story is the beautiful human nature of the people living in this Arcadian Western Hunan. Cuicui is the embodiment of beautiful human nature. Though shining brightly with the radiance of the divine, she pursues a form of life that is "graceful, healthy and natural, and does not go against humanity." Shen Congwen's purpose in exploring human nature and life in this age-old Western Hunan is, by looking back into China's traditional countryside, to find an inner strength that can activate China.

Standing in the opposite direction of the "Beijing School" is the "Shanghai School" led by Zhang Ailing. Zhang Ailing (1921–1995), formerly known as Zhang Ying, was born into an old and well-known family in Shanghai and was well versed in traditional Chinese culture. In 1939, she passed an entrance exam and received a letter of admission from London University. But she did not go to London University because of the Second World War. Instead, she went to Hong Kong University. At the outbreak of the Pacific War in 1942, she returned to Shanghai

Zhang Ailing

from Hong Kong and started working as a professional writer. Her major works include a collection of novellas and short stories, *Legends*, the novels *Predestined Half a Lifetime*, *Reunion*, a collection of prose writings and stories, *Zhang Kan*, and a collection of prose writings, *Gossips*.

Differing from Shen Congwen, who had his eyes on China's rural world, Zhang Ailing focused on modern urban civilization in her writings from beginning to end. All her stories are set against the background of Hong Kong and Shanghai, where millions of men and women, in an age of transition from the old to the new, lead a life that is half Chinese and half Western. The main content of Zhang Ailing's works is about the gloomy life of the city people, and the actual situation and mental state of women from traditional old families in modern society are the focus of her attention. *The Story of the Gold Fetters* (included in *Legends* in 1943), one of Zhang Ailing's major works, tells the story of Cao Qiqiao, a widow from an old feudal family. Cao Qiqiao, the daughter of a sesame oil mill owner, married into the rich Jiang family as the concubine of the second young master. The second young master of the Jiang family dies of bone tuberculosis after giving Cao Qiqiao a son and a daughter. Cao Qiqiao is a woman of low birth and is jeered at and rejected by the Jiang family. Moreover, her married life with the second young master is actually in name only. Cao Qiqiao, becoming very much depressed, develops an ambiguous and subtle relationship

Front cover of the first edition of *Legends* (Shanghai Magazine edition, 1944).

with the third young master of the Jiang family. But the third young master finally walks out on her because of his fear of the feudal ethic codes, and their relationship comes to a fruitless end. This turns this feeble woman into a frantic monster. Cao Qiqiao tries every means to seize all that is due to her name, including money and her children, which finally leads to the death of her daughter-in-law and the breaking-up of her daughter's good marriage. By the time she eventually has got her children, they have become useless opium addicts. The more Cao Qiqiao tries to grab something, the more it is beyond her reach. Like a beast in an iron cage, she fights fiercely, "the angles of the heavy fetters have cut several people into halves, and those who are still alive have lost half-life." The absurdity and bleakness of life is vividly depicted through the story of Cao Qiqiao.

# New Poetry


## Finding a Voice of Their Own

# New Poetry: Finding a Voice of Their Own

Modern Chinese poetry is generally known as new poetry. New poetry is the opposite of "classical poetry" which is written in classical Chinese to a set of strict rules and conventions. The language used in modern poetry is the vernacular language used in people's daily life. For this reason, modern poetry is also known as "free verse written in the vernacular." In February 1917, Hu Shi's "Eight Free Verses Written in the Vernacular" was published on *New Youth*, which marked the birth of new poetry.

The birth of new poetry in China was closely connected with Western poetry. Most of the poets in China's new poetry circles had studied abroad in European countries, the US, or Japan, or were intellectuals who had received similar schooling. The emergence of new poetry in China, where poetry had been the primary form of literature for two to three thousand years, was the outcome of grafting traditional Chinese poetry on Western literature. The immaturity of the new poetry at its early stage of development can be revealed in "Butterflies," one of the early poems by Hu Shi, Ph.D of Columbia University, USA, and leader of the New Culture Movement:

*Two yellow butterflies fly up into the sky, side by side. / But all of a sudden, one flies down, for reasons unknown, / The other left up there alone looks wretched and forlorn. / None is willing to fly up, for loneliness fills up the sky.*

A quick look at European and American poetry in the same period will give us the following impression. In this year, the Irish symbolist poet W. B. Yeats got married and moved to live in a restored tower at Ballylee (Galway), and his writing turned to metaphysics. The French symbolist poet Valéry began to write poems again and published his "The Young Fate." The Austrian poet Rainer Maria Rilke lived in Munich, Germany and finished the first four stanzas of his "Duino Elegies." The English poet T. S. Eliot published his first collection of poems, which included "The Love Song of J. Alfred Prufrock," a poem that inspired modernist poetry. A significant transition from symbolism to modernism was brewing in Western poetry circles.

Modern Chinese poets started their writing under three pressures. First, as a frame of reference, Western poetry exerted some influences on new poetry and at the same time kept it swathed in the trend of world poetry development. Second, though the Chinese poets had cast off the conventional forms of classical Chinese poetry, they still needed to put in much effort in consideration of the choice of material, aesthetic tendency and emotional expression so that they would not assume the responsibility of the world that Chinese intellectuals usually have in mind. Last but not the least, the first thirty years of the development of new poetry turned out to be a period of violent changes in China. Cultural reform, national liberation, and class conflicts made up the theme of the age, and new poetry had to respond to these issues. In the final analysis, how to find their own voice, or how to create poetry masterpieces, became the mission of modern Chinese poetry.

"Ah red candle! 'Do not ask what you reap, ask only what you sow.'" ("Red Candle" by Wen Yiduo) *Ode to Red Candle*, a painting by Wen Lipeng, the son of Wen Yiduo.

The outstanding poets and poetry schools that emerged in these three decades include: in the 1920s, the Romantic School represented by Guo Moruo (1892–1978), the New Moon School represented by Xu Zhimo (1897–1931) and Wen Yiduo (1899–1946), the Symbolism School represented by Li Jinfa (1900–1976),

Feng Zhi (1905–1993); in the 1930s, the Modernism School represented by Dai Wangshu (1905–1950), Bian Zhilin (1910–2000) and He Qifang (1912–1977), Ai Qing (1910–1996), the July School represented by Lü Yuan (1922–2009) and Niu Han (1923–), the Nine Leaves School represented by Mu Dan (1918–1977) and Zheng Min (1920–).

# Guo Moruo: A Destroyer and a Creator

The greatest contribution Guo Moruo made was that the publication of his collection of poems *The Goddesses* in 1921 added a real modernity to new poetry for the first time.

Guo Moruo, formerly known as Guo Kaizhen, was from Leshan, Sichuan. He went to study in Japan in 1914 and returned in 1923 and engaged himself in cultural work. In 1928, he went into exile in Japan because he was wanted by the government. In 1937, leaving his family behind in Japan, he came back to China to join the war of resistance against Japan. He had multiple identities: a poet, a playwright, a historian, an archaeologist, and a calligrapher. Moreover, he was in politics for a long time. He was a controversial person.

*The Goddesses* contains fifty-seven poems, most of which were written when he studied in Japan. At the time the "May 4th" Movement had already begun. But it was Guo Moruo, a young man living far away from home in Japan, who sang in praise of the spirit of the times and brought into play the lyric function of poetry with "the tone of billows and the sound of thunderbolts." Probably because of this distance, Guo Moruo, instead of abandoning himself to the ignorance of social reality, the depression of life, wrote out many poems, magnificent and wild in style, that are self-praising, self-celebrating, and self-reveling. In writing, he followed the principles of Western romanticism and pantheistic thought and took the German poet Johann

On March 18, 1926, members of the "Creators Club" went to teach at Zhongshan University. From left: Wang Duqing, Guo Moruo, Yu Dafu and Cheng Fangwu.

Wolfgang von Goethe as his teacher. He was also influenced by American poet Walt Whitman in particular. In short, passion and imagination make up the basic creed of his poems.

Guo Moruo, along with Yu Dafu and Cheng Fangwu, founded the "Creators Club," but the fact is that his poems center on bringing destruction to the old in the name of creation. "The Heavenly Dog," a poem from *The Goddesses*, is drawn from an ancient story "The Heavenly Dog Eats Up the Sun." But in this poem, Guo Moruo creates the heavenly dog as a lyrical hero "I," dauntless, rebellious, and defiant. Having eaten up the old world, "I" get endless energy. "I" accomplish self-redemption through boisterous destruction. All these tally with the theme of saving the nation from extinction.

*I am a heavenly dog! I eat up the moon, I eat up the sun. / I eat up all the planets, I eat up the universe. / I become what I am! / ... / I peel off my skin, I eat my flesh, I chew my blood, I gnaw my heart and my liver. / I run on my nerve, I run on my spinal marrow, I run on my brains.*

Another important poem in *The Goddesses* is the long poem "Phoenix Nirvana." Based on the story of the phoenix, "collecting scented wood and burning itself, the phoenix gets reborn from the ashes," Guo Moruo creatively combines ancient Egyptian and ancient Chinese legends in "Phoenix Nirvana" to show his resolution of breaking off from the old world and the former self, as well as his expectations and blessings for the new life of the homeland. He explicitly said, "'Phoenix Nirvana' symbolizes my wish for China's rebirth."

Guo Moruo's later works did not reach the height *The Goddesses* attained. Though superficial, exaggerated, and unrefined in lyrical quality, *The Goddesses* can still be considered a founding work of new poetry that started a new age in poetry creation. Guo Moruo took the lead in exhibiting the makings of a great modern poet in China.

# Ai Qing: A Singer of the Land and the Sun

In 1933, the publication of "Dayanhe, My Nurse" by Ai Qing, formerly known as Jiang Haicheng, attracted the attention of poetry circles. Ai Qing wrote this poem while he was in prison because of his engagement in the Left Wing Movement. Dayanhe was Ai Qing's nurse when he was a child, a countrywoman of low origin from Jinhua, Zhejiang. She had no name: "She was named after her home village." Ai Qing's parents left him in the care of Dayanhe for five years and Ai Qing became the foster son of Dayanhe. In this poem, Ai Qing, with profound love, gives a depiction of Dayanhe's miserable life, kind-heartedness, toughness, and Ai Qing's endless praises for and memory of her. Simplicity of language, slow-moving rhythm, and pensive deep feelings give the poem enormous tension. This is the reason why this poem has touched so many people so deeply. More importantly, in the early years of his writing career, Ai Qing had developed a flesh-and-blood tie with the calamitous earth and people, and this has become the basis for his assuming the role of a speaker for the nation and acting as a mature poet selected by history.

The "land" is one of the two images in Ai Qing's poems. His sentimental attachment to, and ardent love for, the land, which

Ai Qing

is filled with symbolic meanings, are vividly expressed in the widely read poem "I Love This Land." The theme of the poem is pretty simple, but the way Ai Qing expresses it is forceful and impressive. The poet is gloomy, yet his meticulous choice of colors and images makes the poem a lot more lucid and lively. This is unique to the style of Ai Qing's poems.

*If I were a bird, / I would sing with my hoarse voice / Of this land buffeted by storms, / Of this river turbulent with our grief, / Of these angry winds ceaselessly blowing, / And of the dawn, infinitely gentle over the woods... / —Then I would die / And even my feathers would rot in the soil.*

*Why are my eyes always brimming with tears? / Because I love this land so deeply...*

The other major image in Ai Qing's poems is "the sun." Ai Qing believes, "Poetry is the message the human race sends to the future; poetry gives the human race the courage to realize their ideals." Ai Qing spent all his life pursuing a bright future, ideals and a better life. In his poems, the sun now and then takes the form of the spring, dawn, flame, or life. In his poem "The Sun," Ai Qing turns his passionate call to the sun into his sincere faith that the human race will have a much brighter future:

*Then my breast / Is torn open by the hands of fire, / My rotten soul / Gets discarded by the river, / And I gain faith once more / In the resurgence of humanity.*

Ai Qing's writing career lasted for a long time and he wrote the best of his poems in the 1930s and 1940s during China's war of resistance against Japanese aggression. Nine collections of his poems were published, including *The North*, *Toward the Sun*, *Open Fields*, *The Torch* and *The Announcement of the Dawn*. Though there was a two-decade-long break in his writing for political reasons, he still wrote some masterpieces, such as "In Praise of Light," in his later years.

# Mu Dan: Richness vs. Rich Suffering

In his poem "Start off," Mu Dan raises a series of questions in a complicated mood to the god in his mind and describes the situation of the modern people as follows: "…and we are converts,/You gave us riches, as well as rich suffering." Throughout his life, Mu Dan waged a life-and-death fight against such fundamental predicaments either in life or poetry writing. The depth, breadth and height he attained in self-examination, reality tracing, philosophical speculation, language innovation, and poetry exploration have gone farther than his predecessors and peers.

Mu Dan, formerly known as Zha Liangzheng, was born in Tianjin. His ancestral home was Haining, Zhejiang. He was both a poet and a first-rank translator. In 1935, he was admitted to the Foreign Languages Department of Tsinghua University. With the outbreak of the war of resistance against Japan, Mu Dan went into exile to the south of China with The National Southwestern Associated University which was made up of Peking University, Tsinghua University and Nankai University. While he studied in The National Southwestern Associated University, he received the baptism of modern Western poetry in an all-round way. The lectures on "Contemporary English Poetry" given by English professor William Empson aroused his admiration for T. S. Eliot and W. H. Auden. In 1942, he gave up his civilian pursuits and joined the Chinese Expeditionary Force, and participated in

Mu Dan

battles against Japan on the Myanmar Battlefield. In 1948, he went to study in the US. After he returned to China in 1952, he started his teaching career in Nankai University and suffered unfair treatment for quite a long time. He died at the age of fifty-six. "Winter" is the last poem he wrote before his death and is universally acknowledged as a masterpiece.

From start to finish, Mu Dan's poems are marked by distinctive features, cool-headed, imposing and vigorous. In the early days of the war of resistance against Japan, he wrote the following lines to describe the unyieldingness of the Chinese nation, "From their sharp eyes, as many as the stars, /Shoot out terrible rays of revenge." ("Beast") In his poem "Praise," his prophetic singing—

*People living in disgrace, people suffering from rickets, / I want to embrace you one by one, with my blood-stained hands, / Because a nation has got to its feet.*

– is still haunted by deep grief. His "Eight Poems" can be considered a completely new type of Chinese love poem. In these poems there is very little direct outpouring of emotion, but sense and speculation between the lines:

*In the process of natural transmutation, / I fall in love with a temporary you. / Even though I cry, turn to ashes, get reborn from the ashes, / My girl, it's just god playing with himself.*

The lyrical protagonists in Mu Dan's poems are unprecedented. The "I" always falls into split, torn-apart, and conflict conditions, where all the modern people's bewilderment about life is brought to the open. The fight between body and soul keeps on going forever. For this reason, paradoxes are used extensively in his poems:

*We are living creatures of the twentieth century, seething in its darkness. / We have machines and systems, but we have no civilizations. / We are capable of complex emotions, but we have nowhere to turn to. / We have a lot of voices, but none is truth. / We come from one conscience, but we all hide it up.*

("Apparitions")

When facing up to the absurdity and emptiness that are innate to human beings, Mu Dan's bravery rests with that he chooses to fight fearlessly as Lu Xun did, but the weapon he uses is life itself. The lyric style he employs is summed up as "metaphorical lyricism that is near to the abstract."

Sometimes it is a challenge for readers to read Mu Dan's poems. But it is incorrect to conclude that Mu Dan's poems are obscure. On the contrary, profundity is what his poems convey to readers. He noted, "Poetry should inerrably express relatively deeper thoughts." So many contents are loaded in his poems. Apart from expressing emotions and speculations, there also exists a harsh reality: "a Browning, a Mauser, a Hand-held III, /or a revolver that penetrates into human bodies," "hoodlums, cheaters, bandits, we are one band/walking along on jumbled streets." Though the language used is clear-cut everyday language and in no way poetic, the thought it conveys is complicated and deep. It is generally agreed that Mu Dan's poem "The Banner," solitary and high-headed, can serve as a portrait of himself:

*You're the heart of everyone, but you're wiser. / You come along with early morning, but suffer at night. / You can tell the joy of freedom.*

Mu Dan's poems are epic and powerful. Not only has he voiced the suffering and struggle of the times, he has also unearthed the bewilderment of human beings. He is a great national poet of China and a great master poet the Chinese nation has contributed to the world.

# Modern Drama

## Birth and Maturing

Originating in Europe, drama was introduced into China as a new art form in the early years of the twentieth century. "The Spring Willows Society" established by a group of Chinese students studying in Japan in 1906 (principle members including Li Shutong, Zeng Xiaogu, Lu Jingruo and Ouyang Yuqian) was the earliest drama group in China. In the following year, the Spring Willows Society staged Western plays *Camille* and *Uncle Tom's Cabin* in Tokyo and created a sensation, starting an upsurge of introducing Western plays in China. Soon after this, the Spring Willows Society also staged these Western plays in China. The Spring Sunshine Society and the Evolution Group, which were established successively in China, also began to stage some new plays that encouraged progression and revolution. *The Pear Seller* by Hong Shen (1894–1955) and *The Locomotion* by Ouyang Yuqian (1889–1962), both written in 1911, were the earliest stage plays created by Chinese writers. This new and unique art form that was close to real life and put stress on political and moralizing functions was known as "new-style drama" at that time in China. New-style drama borrowed ideas from Western drama and used speeches and actions rather than singing and dancing and librettos as the major means of expression. It was a new art form that was different from traditional Chinese operas. However, due to the failure of the "1911 Revolution," new-style drama met restrictions in encouraging progressiveness and revolution. In order to earn their living, professional drama groups turned their focus to staging family plays and mythical plays that promoted feudal ethics with the ends to cater to some people's vulgar tastes. Consequently new-style drama experienced a gradual decline. Although new-style drama lasted for only about ten years from its start in 1907 to its ending in 1918, it had played the important role of "starting a new art form and setting a new course for the future" in the history of modern Chinese drama and laid the foundation for the later development of drama in China.

During the "May 4$^{th}$" Movement, further reforms were made to modern drama on the basis of new-style drama, including using Western drama for reference, highlighting the humanitarian spirit and realism and opposing the old feudal ideological content and platitudinous vulgar forms of expression.

Many drama theories, playwrights and plays were introduced to China from the West, among which Henrik Ibsen had the greatest influence on China's modern drama and playwrights. Moreover, plays by William Shakespeare, Moliere, Bernard Shaw, Oscar Wilde and Anton Chekhov also had a comparatively great impact on China's theatre. The introduction of Western drama into China provided a far-ranging reference for the establishment of modern Chinese drama in concepts, content and form, and performance skills.

Along with the introduction of Western drama and the construction of modern drama theories, a group of drama societies and excellent plays began to appear in China. In September 1921, Wang Zhongxian, Chen Dabei, Shen Yanbing, Zheng Zhenduo and some others founded "People's Theatre Club," the first modern drama club in China since the "May 4$^{th}$" Movement. "People's Theatre Club" follows the literary concept of "for life," believing that drama must reflect the reality of life, reject the degenerated new-style drama and advocate non-commercialized "amateur theatre movement." The Shanghai Dramatists' Association, which was founded in the same year, also played an active part in the "amateur theatre movement." The Shanghai Dramatists' Association was first founded by Ying Yunwei, Gu Jianchen and some others. With Ouyang Yuqian and Hong Shen becoming members, the Shanghai Dramatists' Association became even stronger and exerted a tremendous influence on society. Both the "People's Theatre Club" and the Shanghai Dramatists' Association declared that they were faithful followers of the "May 4$^{th}$" tradition. They emphasized that drama should reflect current social affairs and carry the mission of social enlightenment. Meanwhile, the practical activities of the Shanghai Dramatists' Association laid the foundation for the transition of modern drama from non-professional to professional, which was vital for the development of drama in China.

Practices in modern drama circles promoted the development of script writing. The one-act play *An Important Event in Life* written by Hu Shi (1919) was the first drama script published in literary journals. The characters are thin and pale and the plot is quite simple, but the mode of unfolding issues that attract public attention through drama opened up the creation of plays during the "May 4<sup>th</sup>" Movement. Besides these "problem plays," romantic plays by Tian Han and Guo Moruo and satirical comedies by Ding Xilin, which were marked with different features, also greatly enriched Chinese drama creation in the 1920s.

Various attempts at modern drama were made in the 1920s, but the one who brought modern drama to maturity was Cao Yu, the greatest playwright in modern Chinese literature. Cao Yu (1910–1996), formerly known as Wan Jiabao, was born into a downfallen feudal bureaucratic family in Tianjin. Cao Yu's mother died when he was still a child and he was brought up by his stepmother. As he often went to opera houses with his stepmother, he was acquainted with local operas and new-style plays at an early age. After he entered Nankai High School, he became a member of the Nankai New Theatre in 1925 to rehearse and adapt plays, which

Cao Yu

gave him a lot of stage experience. In 1928 he was admitted to Nankai University. In the following year he was transferred to the Department of Western Literature of Tsinghua University to study Western literature and drama. Upon graduation from university, Cao Yu finished his maiden work *Thunderstorm* and became famous overnight. Later he wrote *Sunrise*, *Wilderness*, and *Beijing People*, which established him as the master playwright in the history of modern Chinese literature.

The birth of *Thunderstorm* (1934) along with some other plays by Cao Yu after the mid-1930s marked the maturity of modern Chinese drama. In writing his plays, Cao Yu used the techniques of expression often found in Western plays and tailored them to China's conditions. By doing so, he succeeded in having stage plays fully express the life and the ethos of the common Chinese people for the first time. Above all, while Cao Yu successfully used the concept of tragedy from classical Western drama, he never moved away from the current social environment. On the contrary, he combined the tragic destiny of the characters and social tragedy.

*Thunderstorm*, a four-act play, is Cao Yu's maiden work, as well as the work that made him famous. It tells of a series of tragedies triggered by an incest incident in an upper class family. Zhou Puyuan, the master of the Zhou family, was in love with the housemaid of his family, Shiping, when he was young, and they gave birth to two sons. Forced by family pressure and succumbing to the feudal tradition, he abandoned Shiping and married Fanyi who was well-matched in social and economic status. The Old Lady of the Zhou's had Zhou Ping, the elder son of Zhou Puyuan and Shiping, remain in the Zhou's house and turned Shiping and the younger son out of the family. In desperation, Shiping had no way out but to drown herself in a river carrying her younger son in her arms. But, fortunately, Shiping and the child did not die. In order to make a living, Shiping married Lu Gui and gave birth to

A still from modern drama *Thunderstorm*.

a daughter, Lu Sifeng. Shiping changed her younger son's name to Lu Dahai. Over ten years later, Lu Gui became the housekeeper and Lu Sifeng became a servant girl of the Zhou's due to a strange combination of circumstances. For many years Zhou Puyuan thought that Shiping and the younger son had drowned and felt very guilty. On the other hand, Zhou Puyuan and Fanyi were cold towards each other. In these circumstances, Fanyi and Zhou Ping fell in love and had an affair. However, Zhou Ping abandoned Fanyi because of his selfish and cowardly character and his guilt at commiting incest, and then fell deeply in love with Lu Sifeng. But Fanyi refused to let him go. One gloomy afternoon when a thunderstorm was coming, Shiping came to the Zhou's mansion to look for Sifeng, but met Zhou Puyuan by chance. Seeing that Shiping was still alive, Zhou Puyuan showed no surprise at the reunion. On the contrary, he thought Shiping had come to him to settle their old accounts. At the same time, Lu Dahai, a miner working for the Zhou's came to Zhou's mansion to argue with Zhou Puyuan about the miners' strike that was then going on. The two sides had a verbal conflict. Zhou Ping, who was also there, gave Lu Dahai two harsh slaps in the face. In the evening, Zhou Ping climbed into Sifeng's room through the windows. Fanyi, who had been tailing Zhou Ping, had the windows bolted by stealth. Shiping and Lu Dahai found Zhou Ping at Sifeng's room and Sifeng ran away in shame. At night, Shiping and Lu Dahai came to Zhou's mansion and learned about the affair between Sifeng and Zhou Ping. At the same time, Fanyi and her son Zhou Chong came to stop Zhou Ping and Sifeng, who were preparing to elope. On hearing the news, Zhou Puyuan showed up too. As he caught sight of Shiping, Zhou Puyuan assumed that she had deliberately come here to let Zhou Ping know she was his mother. Zhou Puyuan asked Zhou Ping to go down on his knees before Shiping and told him Shiping was his mother. By now the truth about the complex relationship between the characters was out and then came the dramatic climax. Feeling terribly ashamed, Sifeng flew out of the house and was struck by lightening in the garden. Zhou Chong also died of an electric shock in an attempt to save her. Zhou Ping shot himself, Shiping and Fanyi went insane, finally leaving Zhou Puyuan living alone in repentance. *Thunderstorm* is a family tragedy, a social tragedy, as well as a tragedy about destiny. In this extended family, some die, some become insane, finally leaving an old man living alone with painful memories. However, the person who has survived and suffered most is none other than the begetter of all these tragedies. Zhou Puyuan is a typical capitalist with a strong mark of feudal thought. When he was young, he succumbed to the feudal ethics and forced Shiping and her son to end up on the streets. Zhou Puyuan's despotic dictatorship in the family is the root of Fanyi's mental anguish. Fanyi, yearning for freedom and wanting to free herself from her present life, takes every chance to hold Zhou Ping, Zhou Puyuan's son, fast to her. Due to Zhou Puyuan's cruel exploitation of the workers and the disintegration of the workers' strike through cheating, his natural son Lu Dahai becomes his sworn enemy. However, most important of all, the play vividly shows people's helplessness against what is decided by fate. The unnatural death of the innocent Lu Sifeng and Zhou Chong speaks well for the ruthlessness of fate.

If Cao Yu's *Thunderstorm* is a sign of maturity in modern drama, Lao She's *Teahouse* (1957) is a testament to the glory of contemporary drama. *Teahouse* is also a world-renowned Chinese play, and has been described as a "Miracle of Oriental Drama."

Using Yutai Teahouse as the setting and three representative eras as the backdrop, *Teahouse*, a three-act play by Lao She, vividly demonstrates changes in Chinese society across half a century. Teahouses in China are places which people from all walks of

A still from the modern drama *Teahouse*.

life love to visit. A teahouse is usually a small community. In this special environment there are all kinds of characters, and the fate of these characters is a reflection of the historical changes of the times. The first act tells about the hardships and suffering of the people after the failure of the "Wuxu Reform" (1898, also known as "Hundred Days Reform") The second act tells about society under the rule of the Northern Warlords after the failure of the "1911 Revolution." The third act reflects the chaotic conditions under the rule of the Kuomintang after the Chinese people's victory in the Sino-Japanese war. "Wuxu Reform," the "1911 Revolution" and the Sino-Japanese war are the major events in the history of China. However, the reform, the revolution, and even the victory in the war resulted in no fundamental change in society or in the people's suffering. After the reform, the revolution, and the war come to an end, darkness and confusion regain ground. The characters in the play either become morally degenerated or fall into even more difficulties. Little Iron Mouth Tang, the son of Iron Mouth Tang the physiognomy practitioner,

Beijing People's Art Theatre created modern theatre art with special Chinese national characteristics.

becomes the "Heavenly Teacher Tang" of a reactionary, superstitious secret society. Little Song Enzi, the son of ruffian Song Enzi, becomes a special agent working for the Kuomintang. Little Pock Face Liu, the son of Pock Face Liu, a trafficker in women, becomes the owner of a brothel. Wang Lifa, however hard and careful he tries to keep teahouse business going, is beyond himself and commits suicide. National capitalist Qin Zhongyi, a faithful believer in "saving the nation by engaging in industry" finally goes bankrupt. The Fourth Elder Chang, a man who earns his own living, also ends up down and out. However the darkness of society will perish one day. The play ends with Wang Lifa, Qin Zhongyi and Fourth Elder Chang scattering ghost money to have the three damnable eras completely buried and left behind.

# Literature in the New Era

## Reflections, Root-seeking and Explorations

# Memories of Historical Wounds

When the Cultural Revolution (1966-1976) came to an end, contemporary literature entered a brand-new historical period. The whole nation's campaign to bring order out of chaos and emancipate thought brought new development opportunities for contemporary literature. The chapter of "ten thousand horses being all muted" and "all flowers dying" in the world of art and literature was closed forever, and the basic policy of "letting a hundred flowers blossom and a hundred schools of thought contend" was restored as the guiding principle in literary writing. A large number of art and literary workers regained their freedom to write and comment, and their works were also revived. Literary circumstances in the new era were completely changed and, as a result, literary production came back to life and quickly flourished. Contemporary Chinese literature continued after a nightmare-like period of ten years.

From the end of the Cultural Revolution to the early 1980s, denouncing and reflecting on the recent past became the mainstay of literary creation. Therefore, writings about the persecution of intellectuals or defilement of the educated youth poured out. Since all the writers had lived through the Cultural Revolution, the stories they told were accounts of their memories of historical wounds. Liu Xinwu's short story *A Teacher in Charge of a Class* (1977) and Lu Xinhua's story *The Scar* (1978) were considered as the start of the telling of these memories. Liu Xinwu's *A Teacher in Charge of a Class* was about two junior high school students—"good student" Xie Huimin and "young rogue" Song Baoqi. Both of them were so misled by the "Gang of Four" (a powerful political clique consisting of Jiang Qing, Zhang Chunqiao, Yao Wenyuan and Wang Hongwen) that their mentality was totally distorted. By telling the story, Liu Xinwu tries to reveal the trauma of the Cultural Revolution for common people, especially the young. Lu Xinhua's story *The Scar*, by revealing the emotional world of a mother and her daughter, denounces the Cultural Revolution as the sole cause of the falling out and final separation of the two as well as of the psychological scars left on the daughter. As a result, the title of the book "Scar" became the synonym for this genre of novels. Scar Literature was the first wave of the trend denouncing and reflecting on the Cultural Revolution. After this first wave came the trend of Introspection Literature. While Scar Literature was the source of Introspection Literature, the latter deepened the former. Based on Scar Literature's revelation and denouncement of the Cultural Revolution, Introspection Literature traced its viewpoint further back in history—from the Cultural Revolution to the mid-1950s, and made a profound criticism of the ultra "leftism" routes followed since 1949, especially since the mid-1950s. This resulted in a more rational, yet more tragic trend in literary writing. Among the writings of this period, Gao Xiaosheng's *Li Dashun Builds a House* (1979) is regarded as the representative work of Introspection Literature. In the novel, a common peasant, Li Dashun, made up his mind to build a house with three rooms but only realized his dream thirty years later. By recounting Li Dashun's sad experience, the novel made a profound reflection on experiences and lessons drawn from the thirty years since 1949 and discussed the deep-rooted sources of "left-deviationist" mistakes.

There were two groups of contemporary writers who wrote about memories of historical wounds. One group was the writers who had suffered from assault or persecution in the 1950s, including Wang Meng, Zhang Xianliang and Gao Xiaosheng. These writers were nurtured in the "May 4th" literature and influenced by Western culture. At the same time, they accepted the left wing literary notion that literature should serve politics. After more than twenty years of hardship, they quite naturally chose their own life experiences and took up their pens again after long years of suspension.

Wang Meng's works on the Cultural Revolution included *The Most Valuable, Cousin, Bolshevik Salute, The Butterfly, The Variegated Color, Voice of Spring, Dream of the Sea,* and *The Strain of Meeting*. These works turned away from the sentimental and sorrowful tones of Scar Literature and focused instead on human nature itself. The theme of these works tends to reveal the complex relationship between intellectuals who plunged into revolution when young and the ideal society to which they devoted

Wang Meng

themselves. Take *Bolshevik Salute,* for example. Zhong Yicheng, the protagonist, became a revolutionary in boyhood and devoted his youth and passion to the realization of communism. This ideal society, however, did not give this devotee sufficient confidence in return. Instead, it poured sufferings on him. This conflict plunged him into total confusion.

Zhang Xianliang's works on historical wounds often reflected his experiences and thus had autobiographical features too. These works included *Flesh and Soul, Mimosa* and *Half of Man is Woman,* among others. Zhang Xianliang was persecuted as a rightist in the 1950s and sent to a labor-reform farm in northwest China. Most of the protagonists in his works also bore images of abandoned intellectuals who were sent to bleak and desolate places for labor reform. The protagonists were in constant hunger for food, sex, and spirituality. While going through hardship, the protagonists finally found power and impetus from the laborers at the lowest rung, especially from kind-hearted and capable women. Through this process, the protagonists overcame their sufferings and elevated their spirits to a higher level. Zhang Xianliang's novels possess a profound rational feature due to their philosophical explorations into human spirits and human life.

Apart from *Li Dashun Builds a House*, his representative work of Introspection Literature, Gao Xiaosheng also created the "Chen Huansheng novel series" including *The Funnel House-holder*, *Chen Huansheng's Adventure in Town*, *Chen Huansheng Changes His Job*, and *Chen Huansheng's Adventure Abroad*. All these novels depict realistically the historical shift of peasants' life after 1949, reflected thoroughly on the experiences and lessons of the ultra "leftism," and reveal the deep-rooted political, economic, and historical reasons bringing about their miserable fate. At the same time, the novels vividly illustrate the changes in peasants' character and mentality in the new era of opening up and reform.

The other group of contemporary writers who wrote about historical wounds was the educated youth who went to live and work in the countryside during the Cultural Revolution. Similar to the writers who picked up their pen again after the Cultural Revolution, this group of writers injected autobiographical elements into their works. Nevertheless, due to differences in circumstance and status between the two groups, each group had their respective inclinations in writing. The writers persecuted in the 1950s re-entered the literary world and became cultural elites. In contrast, the educated youth went out from cities to the fields to accept "reeducation" when they should have been educated in school. They returned to the cities after the Cultural Revolution, yet new problems and confusion arose. As a result, while the writers who made a comeback onto the literary stage focused on the exploration of historical events through the fate of individuals characters, the educated youth were more concerned with retrieving their lost youth and dreams. Therefore, this genre of writing is usually referred to as "Literature of the Educated Youth." Later, "Literature of the Educated Youth" falls into two categories: one of them denounced the "Down to the Countryside Movement," criticizing the absurdity of life in that period. The other category, however, frequently recalled the countryside life, seeking value in that experience. The novels of this category either emphasized enthusiasm, sincerity, and the spirit of sacrifice, creativity, and responsibility in the educated youth, or dug into the humanity of rural life to create peace in their minds.

# Root-Seeking and Countryside Literature

In the 1980s, Root-Seeking Literature became the mainstay in the literary world. Han Shaogong's essay "The Roots of Literature" (1985) was well received upon publication. This triggered a large-scale "root-searching movement in literature." The movement intended to reshape the self-image of the Chinese nation and to seek the probability of the re-establishment of Chinese traditional culture by inquiring into the Chinese traditional culture and exploring the contents with modern characteristics in ancient Chinese culture. As for novel creations, specific cultural-historical areas, original lifestyles of specific nationalities, or traditional values were the main themes. Jia Pingwa's "Shang Zhou" novel series reflecting the Shaanxi Plain culture and Li Hangyu's "Gechuanjiang" novel series about Wu-Yue culture were all excellent novels produced under the root-seeking movement in literature.

In fact, Root-Seeking Literature can be traced back to the novels created in the early 1980s by such writers as Wang Zengqi, Deng Youmei, Wu Ruozeng, and their novels such as *Buddhist Initiation, Na Wu* and *The Jadeite Cigarette Holder*. The publication

Wang Zengqi

of Wang Zengqi's *Buddhist Initiation* in 1980 found an echo in the literary world with its new writing style. The novel mainly tells of the experiences of the young Minghai who lived in Biqi Buddhist Temple as a little monk. The novel had descriptions of the subtle love of Minghai for the maiden Yingzi during their stay together as well as the monks' earthly lives of singing love songs and getting married. In the temple, the commandments for monks were not taken so seriously, for it was believed there that being a monk was just a career, no different from any other. Therefore, monks there lived an earthly life and they could kill pigs, eat meat, play cards or mahjong just as the civilians did. This novel is a poetic portrayal of the local conditions and customs of the specific region, representing people's aspirations and pursuit of healthy and natural humanity. This kind of writing style was unique at the time and provided much inspiration for writers in following years.

So far as Chinese traditional culture is concerned, Han Shaogong adopted an aesthetic standard different from Wang Zengqi and the others. Han Shaogong's works were more critical, for the reestablishment of the national spirit and to locate the root causes that had hindered the progress of national culture. In Han Shaogong's novel *Bababa*, the Jitou Stockade represented the symbolic image of inherent weakness of Chinese culture. The Jitou Stockade was located in a remote mountainous area, and the enclosed and isolated natural environment created the breeding ground for primitive superstition, ignorance, and brutality. The combination of the environment and culture formed a vicious cycle, resulting in the stagnation of the Jitou Stockade since ancient times. Han Shaogong amplified the Jitou Stockade's ignorance and brutality by using hyperbole and distortion just for the purpose of its salvation. For this reason, the novel became an important work in the Root-Seeking Literature.

If Han Shaogong's *Bababa* is treated as an inquiry into ancient national culture for the root causes hindering the progress of that culture, Zhang Chengzhi's *Rivers in the North* should be viewed as a spiritual journey by tracking the course of ancient national culture. The rivers as described in the novel, the Yellow River, the Yongding River, Huangshui River, as well as the rivers recalled as Heilongjiang River and Eerqisihe River, finally converged into one, which symbolized national culture and national spirit. Individuals' ideals and youth gained their values and meanings with the river gushing down. The combination of individual fate with that of the country and the Chinese nation was the basic theme in Zhang Chengzhi's novels. The idealism and romanticism found along with a relaxing flow of poetic sentiment are Zhang Chengzhi's prominent strengths.

Of all the novels of the "Root-Seeking Literature," Jia Pingwa's and Mo Yan's novel creations are most worthy of mention. Since 1983, Jia Pingwa's "Shang Zhou" novel series have been the main achievement in the trend of "Root-Seeking Literature." In the "Shang Zhou" novel series, Jia Pingwa dug deep into his hometown—Danfeng County, Shang Zhou, Shaanxi Province. By portraying the life changes of the locals, Jia Pingwa presented the clashes between indigenous traditional values and the transformation of the time, as well as happiness, anger, grief, and joy in the clashes.

While Jia Pingwa's writings concentrated on the peasants' confusion and dramatic changes in face of the reform and opening up in the real world, Mo Yan's *Red Sorghum* series focused on an imaginary rural world. In the series, Mo Yan made up the world of "Gaomi Northeast Township" and narrated the legends and stories happening there. The novel *Red Sorghum* (1986) is about "My grandpa"—his anti-Japanese story and his love story with "My grandma." The novel truly reflects the peasants' cultural mentality and character. The peasants possess many conflicting qualities such as "the prettiest and the ugliest, the most other-worldly and the most mundane, the most sacred and the most profane, the most heroic and the most contemptible, the most hard-drinking and the most romantic," representing great vitality. In the anti-Japanese war, this vitality sublimated and became the indomitable and dauntless national spirit.

# Avantgarde Novels

With the detachment of literature from social-politics, writing stepped into an experimental stylistic shift from "what to write" to "how to write." This experimental writing style, with an emphasis on the narrative style or paradigm, was the main feature of Avantgardist novels. The representative figures were Ma Yuan, Yu Hua, Su Tong, Ge Fei and Sun Ganlu.

Published in 1984, Ma Yuan's *The Goddess of Lhasa River* was the first novel that emphasized the importance of narrative strategies. After this, a series of stories set in Tibet, such as *The Lure from Gandise* and *Fabrication,* all bore ostensible features of Avantgarde novels in their narrative style. Ma Yuan's experiment with narrative style triggered the revolution in narration of the mid- and late 1980s. Without giving much stress to the content and meaning of the stories, Ma Yuan's novels placed, instead, narrative techniques as their supreme goal. His novels usually crossed boundaries between reality and imagination. In neither real nor imaginary settings, the novels cross-told several unrelated stories or clips of stories. This was a break from the traditional pursuit of content and meaning in novel writing and left its mark on the literary world.

1987

The most distinctive feature of Yu Hua's novels was their "indifferent narrative." The novelist, from an outsider's point of view, described death and violence with a completely indifferent tone. Through the "indifferent narrative," the novels presented a "false form" contrary to the real world and daily life. The novelette *One Kind of Reality* (1988) could be regarded as the masterpiece of Yu Hua. It is about the vendetta of two brothers—Shangang and Shanfeng. Pipi, Shangang's son accidentally dropped his

In the mid- and late 1980s, literature magazine *Harvest* published numerous stories by Avantgardists.

cousin, Shanfeng's son, on the ground and the latter died. In a rage, Shanfeng kicked Pipi to death. Then the elder brother Shangang killed his younger brother Shanfeng himself and was finally sentenced to death. The soul-stirring family disaster was narrated in a calm and normal tone and the bloody slaughter between the two brothers was described in minute detail. This narrative style was a sharp contrast to traditional novel writing ethics and showed ostensible features of Avantgardist works.

In contrast to other Avantguardists, Su Tong's works embodied harmony of narrative skills and the plot. In experimenting with new forms of style, he did not refrain from striving for a moving story. Su Tong's best-known novels were the "Red Powder Series," including *Wives and Concubines*, *Blush* and *Women's Lives*. Among these novels, *Wives and Concubines* was created in the framework of an old feudal family where four women lived together with one man. The novelist tried to explore the difficult living conditions and the psychology of these women. It was about the traditional rivalry between wives and concubines in trying to win a man's favor. Yet, in the novel, this rivalry added to women's severe struggle for survival. Under this circumstance, the women's complex, venomous, perverse mentality and their cruel infightings were startling. Su Tong's novels were mainly based on historical stories. While the novelist was keenly recounting erotic stories of the old times, he was also unveiling an aesthetic taste of the traditional writers.

Among all the Avantgardists, the focus of Ge Fei's novels was also mainly on the stories of the old times. Yet, in seemingly classical narration, the climax of a traditional novel was deliberately omitted. Take *The Lost Boat* for example. It described a love story which happened during a period of tangled warfare between warlords. Just before a war, Brigadier Xiao met his old love Xing in a small village and their love came to burn again. At this time, however, Xing had already married the castrator of village—Sanshun. The latter discovered the secret love between the two and castrated Xino. Xino was sent back to her mother's in Yu Guan. Xiao then followed Xing to Yu Guan, only to be shot dead by one of his guards on his return. What Xiao really did in Yu Guan, as the crucial part of the whole plot, was unexpectedly omitted. This structural omission was deliberately designed to create a slot in narration. The novel has, therefore, been deemed a model of the experimental style typical of Avantguardists.

## Neo-Realism

While the novels of "Neo-Realism" were created at the same time as the Avantgardist novels, or just a little later, these writings became influential in 1989. Neo-Realist novels were once considered a revival of realist writings, yet they were quite different from contemporary realist novels. Neo-Realist novels did not, as expected, portray typical characters and typical circumstances as well as social-historical natures. On the contrary, they focused their critical viewpoint on the mediocre and earthly lives of common people, presented the hardship and loneliness of individuals whose trivial life was brimming with troubles and desires. Basically, Neo-Realist novels adopted an objective narrative style with very little interference from the novelists. The leading figures of Neo-Realism were Chi Li, Fang Fang, Liu Zhenyun and Liu Heng.

Chi Li's *Troubled Life* and Fang Fang's *The Scenery* are two representative works of Neo-Realism. Chi Li's *Troubled Life* and next two novels—*Apart From Love* and *Sunrise*-constitute Chi Li's "Neo-realist trilogy." *Troubled Life* portrays a mediocre and trifling day of an ordinary worker—Yin Jiahou. The novelette is a detailed recount of the protagonist's life troubles within a day. The story starts with the protagonist's child falling out of bed in the second half of the night, followed by the morning's queuing for the tap and the bathroom, competing for space on a crowded bus with the child, finding third-prize award money on arriving at the workplace, getting on a crowded bus and coming back home from work with his child, doing household chores after getting home and so on. The story does not end until he goes to bed at half past eleven at night. The novel tells the life story as it happens, focusing on trivia, the common way of life and difficult living conditions and thus possessing all the basic features of Neo-Realist novels. The meaning of the novel goes far beyond that, because Yin Jiahou's one day in the novel is an epitome of

Chi Li

his whole life. Yin Jiahou's personal troubles are a portrait of the troubles of Chinese common people in that period. Therefore, Yin Jiahou's life troubles are the troubles of a whole generation. Fang Fang is another leading novelist of Neo-Realism, whose masterpiece *The Scenery* describes the grey life of a several-child family, an incisive reflection of the humble, tough living conditions of the urban people at the bottom of the social ladder.

In contrast to the novels of other Neo-Realists, Liu Zhenyun's writings tend to explore the deep-rooted absurdity and dissimilation of humanity through unveiling the mediocre and superficial phenomena in daily life. In his novel *Chicken Feathers Everywhere* (1991), Liu Zhenyun, in a somewhat teasing and ironic tone, depicts the trivia in the life of Xiaolin, a civil servant, vividly displaying the pessimistic life of many common people under the heavy pressure of trivialities and heavy burden of life. "Mediocre and trifling life is tough. The toughness does not mean that you must climb a mountain of swords or plunge into a sea of flames. Undergoing these severe trials is not so tough. What is tough is the day-after-day and year-after-year trifles in life." (Liu Zhenyun) It is the seemingly insignificant trivia that wears away the youth and passion of those like Xiaolin and begets their submission to powerful mundane orders and satisfaction with a mediocre life.

# New Poetry

In the literature of the new era, "Misty Poetry" was an influential trend in poetry with prominent artistic achievement. Drawing mainly on the writing techniques of modernist poetry in Western countries, "Misty Poetry" emphasized the adoption of such techniques as symbols, hints, associations and distortions, reflected its aesthetic features of obscurity and multi-interpretation, expressed the poets' reflection on human nature and self-value and their longing for spiritual freedom as well as their serious criticism about and doubt over reality. The most important Misty poets include Bei Dao, Shu Ting, Gu Cheng, Jiang He, and Yang Lian.

The publication of Bei Dao's poem "The Answer" in *Poetry Monthly*, the official poetry journal, in March 1979 marked the birth of Misty Poetry. "The Answer" is a venting of criticism about, and total denial of, the period of time when a generation of young people came to realize they had been fooled and hurt during the Cultural Revolution. Bei Dao's poems are pervasive with sharp criticism about reality and a strong sense of crisis. He does not shun the darkness or ugliness of the real world, and denounces and exposes the reality in a critical and challenging manner. This is the most distinctive feature of Bei Dao's poems.

Shu Ting was a contemporary of Bei Dao. In contrast to the intrepid masculinity in Bei Dao's poems, Shu Ting's verses are filled with exquisite female features. "Missing You" (1978) and "The Double-Masted Boat" (1979) are considered her masterpieces. By depicting a fruitless love, the poem "Missing You"presents a delicate sentiment of bitter sweetness. And "The Double-Masted Boat" expresses the interdependent as well as independent relationships between two lovers. Shu Ting was inclined to choose love as themes for her poems. Yet, she succeeded in revealing her awareness and concerns over social reality while describing love in her poems, so her poems are short of social connotation and rich humanity. This successful combination of "the individual" with

Poet Bei Dao at the "Survivors Poetry Reading" in the spring of 1989.

"the collective" is also a salient feature of Shu Ting's other poems.

Gu Cheng is a poet of strong character among the Misty poets. Being referred to as a "Poet of Fairytales," Gu Cheng was intent on creating an elegant and pure world of fairytales in his poems, and using an ideal world created in his poems as a foil for the darkness and ugliness in the real world. At the same time, Gu Cheng was very good at capturing and presenting perceptions in his poems.

Apart from the above-mentioned poets, Jiang He and Yang Lian are also taken as important Misty poets.

In the wake of the Misty poets, a group of younger poets with higher educational backgrounds entered the world of poetry. These younger poets took Misty poems as their targets to surpass, issued manifestos on poetry and practiced poetry writing and formed a new trend in poetry. This group of poets is collectively

*Today* magazine is the major base for new poetry.

called the Third Generation Poets. Prior to this, two generations of poets were born after 1949. The first generation of poets was represented by Gong Liu, Shao Yanxiang and Bai Hua who entered the poetry circles in the 1950s. The second generation of poets was the Misty poets with Bei Dao and Shu Ting as the representatives. The Third Generation Poets attempted to break the poetic regulations set by Misty Poetry with their own poetic creations, and to build a new series of poetic creation criteria of their own. The general features of the Third Generation poems are antihero, anti-loftiness, and civilianization, which embody the awakening of the Third Generation Poets' awareness of the populace. In alignment with these features is the poets' employment of such techniques as anti-image, anti-rhetoric, and colloquialism in poetic creation, which further reflects the poets' shift of value orientation to appreciation of ugliness. This is a major feature of Third Generation Poetry's experiments with poetic language, and a practice of its advocacy of "poetry takes language as its goal, poems end in language."